SINGER

SEWING REFERENCE LIBRARY®

Decorative Machine Stitching

Contents

Copyright © 1990
Cy DeCosse Incorporated
5900 Green Oak Drive
Minnetonka, Minnesota 55343
1-800-328-3895
All rights reserved
Printed in U.S.A.

Also available from the publisher: *Sewing
Essentials, Sewing for the Home, Clothing Care
& Repair, Sewing for Style, Sewing Specialty
Fabrics, Sewing Activewear, The Perfect Fit,
Timesaving Sewing, More Sewing for the Home,
Tailoring, Sewing for Children, Sewing with
an Overlock, 101 Sewing Secrets, Sewing Pants*

*That Fit, Quilting by Machine, Creative
Sewing Ideas, Sewing Lingerie, Sewing Projects
for the Home*

Library of Congress
Cataloging-in-Publication Data

Decorative machine stitching.

  p.cm. — (Singer sewing reference library)
ISBN 0-86573-255-8
ISBN 0-86573-256-6 (pbk.)
1. Machine sewing. 2. Embroidery, Machine.
3. Lace and lacemaking.   4. Machine
appliqué.   I. Cy DeCosse Incorporated.
II. Series.
TT713.D38   1990   90-32957
646.2'044 — dc20   CIP

Distributed by: Contemporary Books, Inc.
  Chicago, Illinois

CY DE COSSE INCORPORATED
Chairman: Cy DeCosse
President: James B. Maus
Executive Vice President: William B. Jones

DECORATIVE MACHINE STITCHING
Created by: The Editors of Cy DeCosse
  Incorporated, in cooperation with the
  Sewing Education Department, Singer
  Sewing Company. Singer is a trademark
  of The Singer Company and is used
  under license.

Executive Editor: Zoe A. Graul
Technical Director: Rita C. Opseth

SINGER

SEWING REFERENCE LIBRARY®

Decorative
Machine Stitching

Cy DeCosse Incorporated
Minnetonka, Minnesota

Project Managers: Linda Halls, Ann Schlachter
Senior Art Director: Lisa Rosenthal
Writer: Rita C. Opseth
Editors: Janice Cauley, Bernice Maehren
Sample Coordinator: Carol Olson
Technical Photo Director: Bridget Haugh
Sewing Staff: Wendy Fedie, Phyllis Galbraith, Bridget Haugh, Sara Holmen, Julie Muschamp, Linda Neubauer, Lori Ritter, Kari Shoutz, Nancy Sundeen, Barb Vik
Fabric Editor: Joanne Wawra
Photo Studio Manager: Cathleen Shannon
Assistant Photo Studio Manager: Rebecca DaWald
Director of Photography: Tony Kubat

Photographers: Rex Irmen, John Lauenstein, Bill Lindner, Mark Macemon, Charles Nields, Mette Nielsen, Cathleen Shannon
Production Manager: Jim Bindas
Assistant Production Managers: Julie Churchill, Amelia Merz
Production Staff: Joe Fahey, Kevin D. Frakes, Melissa Grabanski, Mark Jacobson, Yelena Konrardy, Daniel Meyers, Linda Schloegel, Greg Wallace, Nik Wogstad
Consultants: Cindy Curtis, Patricia Doty, Kathy Ghorashi, Pamela Hastings, Meta Hoge, Karen Kauffeld, Julie Muschamp, Ann Price, Don Ringstrom, Patsy Shields, Nancy Sundeen

Contributors: Burda Patterns, Inc., Capitol Imports, Inc., Clotilde, Inc., Coats & Clark, Inc., Curtis-Swann, Exotic Silks, Gingher®, Inc., Hi Fashion Fabrics, "Nancy" by Carol Hoffnagle, Laces & Lacemaking-Lace Crafts, Sandra McCormick by Constance Kay, Nancy's Notions®, One + One Designs, Speed Stitch, Inc., Sulky of America, Swiss-Metrosene, Inc., Victorian Treasures, Vogue/Butterick Patterns, YLI Corporation
Color Separations: Scantrans
Printing: Arcata Graphics Company (1091)

Introduction

The sewing machine can be used to embellish garments and home furnishings in many different ways. Some machines offer stitches that are decorative, including utility stitches and automatic decorative stitch patterns. Even the basic straight stitch and zigzag stitch can be used to create special decorative effects. This book will give you ideas for decorative stitching along with step-by-step instructions to ensure successful results.

In Getting Started, you will be shown how to vary the look of the stitches by using specialty needles and threads. You will learn how to perfect the quality of the stitches by using hoops and stabilizers and by adjusting the sewing machine tension.

The Basic Stitches section includes tips for perfect topstitching, satin stitching, and couching. You will also learn how to sew with specialty threads in the bobbin of the machine for special effects.

In the Appliqués section of the book, you will learn how to sew several types of appliqués. The type you select will depend on the look you want to create, the fabrics you are using, and whether you want a supple appliqué or one that has more body. Step-by-step instructions are included for each method. There are also tips for pucker-free sewing and for satin stitching around the corners and curves of appliqués. Several ideas for designing and embellishing appliqués are also included in this section.

Some types of decorative stitching that were once done by hand can now be duplicated with machine stitching. In the Heirloom Sewing section, you will learn how to sew cutwork, pintucks, fagoting, and hemstitching by machine. Also learn French machine sewing, which combines many forms of decorative stitching in a single project. Included in the instructions for each heirloom technique is information on the best fabrics to use and the correct presser foot and needle type.

The Free-motion Sewing section of the book takes you beyond the basics of machine-guided sewing and built-in decorative stitches. Learn to stitch with free motion, guiding the fabric by hand without the use of the presser foot and feed dogs. Because free-motion sewing involves new skills, simple practice designs are included to teach the basic free-motion techniques. Use these basic techniques for thread painting, thread sketching, monogramming, or making Battenberg lace.

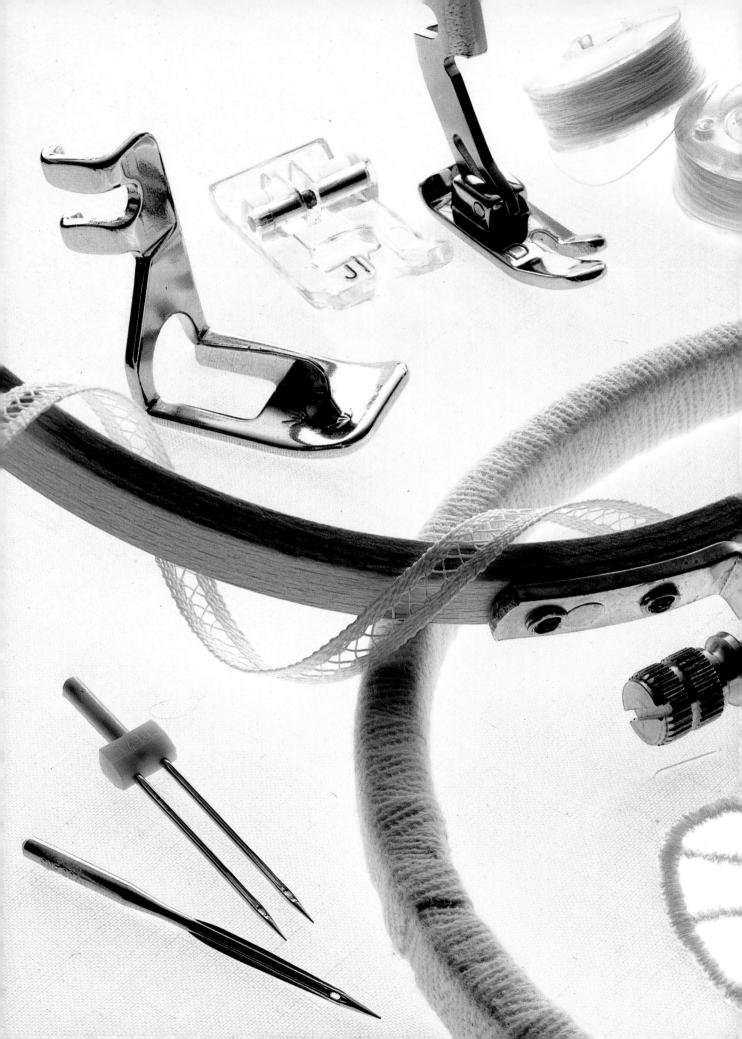

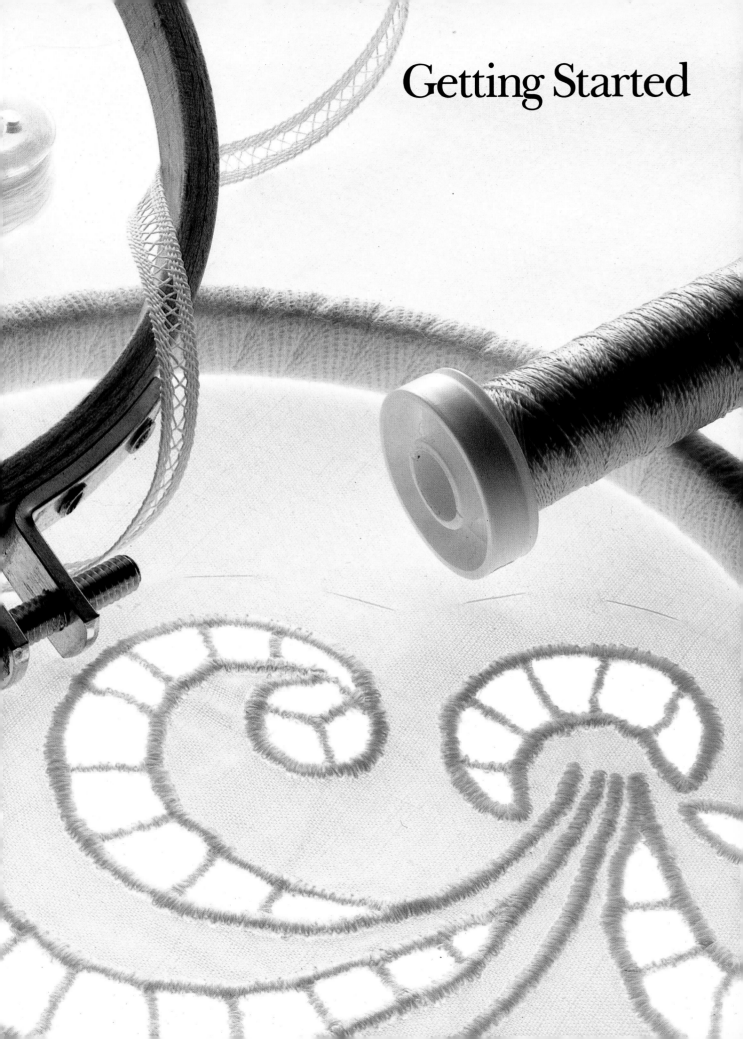

Getting Started

Guide to
Decorative Stitching

There are many types of decorative stitching, offering a wide variety of decorative effects. Use this guide to quickly identify each type of stitching and to determine the correct stitches and accessories to use. Specialty presser feet (page 15) and unique sewing machine needles (page 16) are used for some of the stitching techniques.

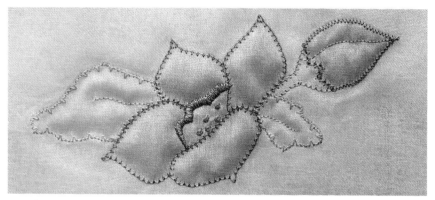

Appliqués, shadow (pages 58 to 63), are designs made up of small pieces of fabrics placed under a sheer overlay and outlined with decorative stitching.

Stitch type: Straight, zigzag, blindstitch, or blanket
Presser foot: Special-purpose or open-toe
Needle: Regular

Battenberg lace (pages 115 to 125) is made by shaping Battenberg tape and embellishing the open areas with free-motion stitching.

Stitch type: Straight and zigzag
Presser foot: None
Needle: Regular

Appliqués (pages 38 to 67) are designs made up of small pieces of fabrics outlined with satin stitching.

Stitch type: Straight and zigzag
Presser foot: Special-purpose or open-toe
Needle: Regular

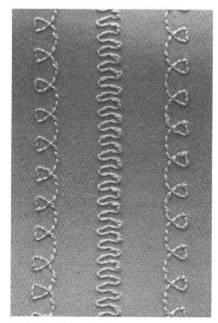

Bobbin thread, decorative (pages 34 and 35), creates a special effect by using specialty thread in the bobbin and stitching with fabric placed right side down.

Stitch type: Straight, zigzag, or other
Presser foot: Special-purpose or open-toe
Needle: Regular

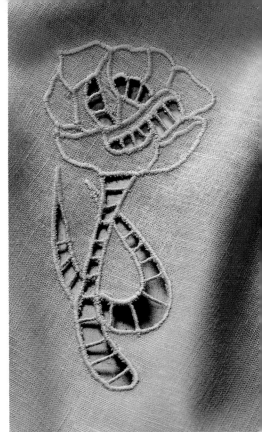

Couching (pages 32 and 33) is attaching narrow trims or heavy threads by stitching over them with decorative stitches.

Stitch type: Zigzag, blanket, blindstitch, or other
Presser foot: Cording or special-purpose
Needle: Regular

Cutwork (pages 72 to 75) has open design areas that are outlined with satin stitching.

Stitch type: Straight and zigzag
Presser foot: Special-purpose or open-toe
Needle: Regular

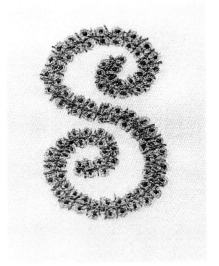

Fagoting (pages 76 to 79) creates an open, lacelike effect at seamlines.

Stitch type: Fagoting, three-step zigzag, or zigzag
Presser foot: Open-toe or tacking
Needle: Regular

Free-motion monograms (pages 109 to 113) are letters formed using free-motion stitching techniques (pages 100 to 105).

Stitch type: Zigzag
Presser foot: None
Needle: Regular

11

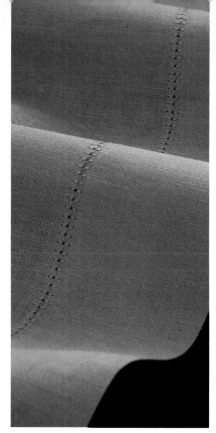

French machine sewing (pages 88 to 97) consists of strips of fabrics and trims joined together. The fabric strips are embellished using several decorative techniques.

Stitch type: Depends on method
Presser foot: Depends on method
Needle: Depends on method

Hemstitching (pages 81 to 85) creates the look of entredeux when sewing hems and attaching lace.

Stitch type: Zigzag, blanket, or other
Presser foot: Special-purpose or open-toe
Needle: Single-wing or double-wing

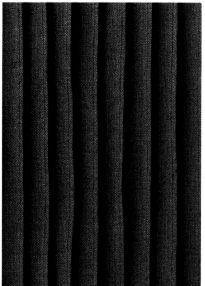

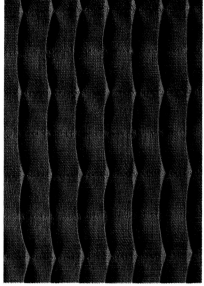

Pintucks, decorative (pages 86 and 87), are formed by stitching near a fold, using a decorative stitch.

Stitch type: Narrow decorative
Presser foot: Special-purpose or open-toe
Needle: Regular

Pintucks, traditional (pages 86 and 87), are formed by stitching near a fold, using straight stitching.

Stitch type: Straight
Presser foot: Straight-stitch
Needle: Regular

Pintucks, twisted (pages 86 and 87), are formed by stitching across traditional pintucks to twist them.

Stitch type: Straight
Presser foot: Straight-stitch
Needle: Regular

Satin stitching (pages 30 and 31) is a solid row of closely spaced zigzag stitches used to stitch decorative design lines, finish edges, apply appliqués, and outline cutwork.

Stitch type: Zigzag
Presser foot: Special-purpose or open-toe
Needle: Regular

Thread sketching and thread painting (pages 106 and 107) both use free-motion stitching techniques (pages 100 to 105) to resemble hand embroidery stitches.

Stitch type: Straight and zigzag
Presser foot: None
Needle: Regular

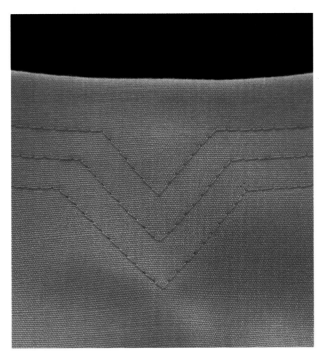

Topstitching (page 27) is used to emphasize the edge of a garment or other design lines, such as seamlines, or to add new design lines.

Stitch type: Straight
Presser foot: Straight-stitch, blindstitch, or topstitching
Needle: Regular

Twin-needle stitching (pages 28 and 29) makes two rows of stitches in one step. Twin-needle stitching can be used to make pintucks.

Stitch type: Straight
Presser foot: Special-purpose, open-toe, or pintuck
Needle: Twin

Specialty Threads

Specialty threads can enhance decorative stitching. Several types of thread, ranging from fine machine embroidery threads to heavier pearl cottons and topstitching threads, can be used successfully in the needle and bobbin of the machine.

Not all specialty threads work well in all sewing machines. You may need to do some testing to see which threads give the best results. It may be necessary to adjust the needle and bobbin tensions of the machine (pages 18 and 19) when using a specialty thread.

Topstitching thread (1) is a heavier thread, used to make the stitches more noticeable. As the name implies, it is frequently used for topstitching.

Metallic thread (2) is available in several weights. The finer metallic threads can be used for machine embroidery; the heavier weights can be used as the cord for couching.

Pearl thread (3) may be cotton or rayon, and it is available in several weights. Depending on the weight, one or more strands can be couched over, or used as the cord for corded satin stitching.

Fine monofilament nylon thread (4) can be used in the bobbin of the machine, so the bobbin thread will not show on the right side. It can also be used for couching over decorative trims, so it does not detract from the trim.

Ribbon thread (5), a flat, lightweight ribbon, can be used in the bobbin of the machine; for decorative stitching, the fabric is placed right side down on the machine. Ribbon thread can also be used as the cord for couching.

Machine embroidery thread (6) is used for smooth, even satin stitching and machine embroidery. Cotton machine embroidery thread, available in weights ranging from 30-weight to 60-weight, gives a matte finish with only a subtle sheen; rayon thread, in 30-weight or 40-weight, has a shiny appearance. Select a fine, lightweight thread for sewing on lightweight fabric and to prevent thread buildup. A heavier thread may be used to achieve good coverage with fewer stitches.

Cotton basting thread (7), a lightweight, inexpensive thread, may be used in the bobbin, when machine embroidery thread is used in the needle. (Photo shows cotton basting thread on wrong side of fabric.)

Presser Feet

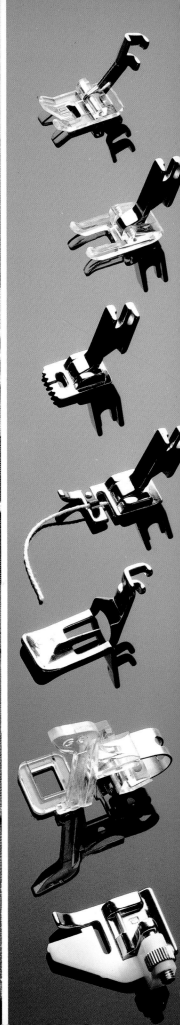

Several presser feet are available, each designed for a specific purpose. Some of these presser feet come with the sewing machine; others may need to be purchased separately.

Special-purpose foot (1), or embroidery foot, is used for satin stitching and machine embroidery. The foot has a wide groove on the bottom, which allows the fabric to feed through the machine smoothly, even with the buildup of heavy decorative stitching. The bar between the toes of the presser foot keeps the fabric smooth as it is fed under the needle.

Open-toe foot (2) is used for sewing intricate design details with corners or curves. The space between the toes of the presser foot allows you to see stitching lines more clearly. The open-toe foot has a groove on the bottom, so it can be used for satin stitching and machine embroidery.

Pintuck foot (3) is used for twin-needle pintucks. There are several grooves on the bottom of the pintuck foot, which keep multiple rows of pintucks an equal distance apart.

Cording foot (4) is used for applying a cord to fabric. The cord is threaded through a hole in the cording foot and feeds automatically during stitching.

Tacking foot (5) is used to make the looped stitches that create fagoting.

Darning foot (6) is used for free-motion machine embroidery, including monogramming and thread painting. Although free-motion embroidery can be done without a presser foot, the darning foot makes it easier to follow the curves of the design.

Blindstitch foot (7), sometimes called a topstitching foot, can be used as a guide for topstitching.

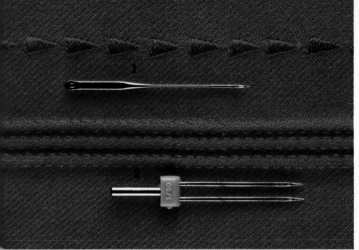

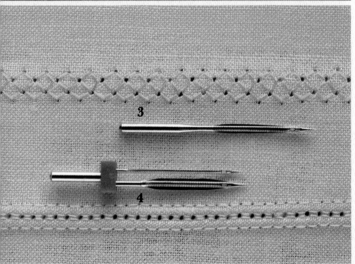

Specialty Needles

For decorative stitching, it is important to use a sharp, new needle. A slightly damaged or a dull needle can cause broken threads and skipped stitches.

A regular needle **(1)** in size 70/9 or 80/11 is used for sewing with fine fabric and thread. To prevent strip-back when using rayon machine embroidery thread, it may be necessary to use a needle one size larger. Strip-back is frayed thread that bunches up at the eye of the needle; it usually occurs when sewing fast.

A twin needle **(2)**, or double needle, is used for sewing two parallel rows of topstitching. When combined with the pintuck foot (page 15), a twin needle is also used for pintucks and corded decorative sewing.

Single-wing **(3)** and double-wing **(4)** needles are used for hemstitching to produce the characteristic "holes" of hemstitched fabric. The double-wing needle features a wing needle and a regular needle on one shank.

Embroidery Hoops

For many types of decorative sewing, it is helpful to place the fabric in an embroidery hoop. The hoop holds the fabric taut so it does not pucker when it is stitched. A 5" to 7" (12.5 to 18 cm) hoop is a good size for most projects.

A wooden hoop with a fixing screw works best for free-motion embroidery because it can be tightened firmly. Select a hoop that is ¼" (6 mm) thick so it will slide easily under the sewing machine needle. The hoop should be very smooth, with beveled edges, so it does not snag the fabric or scratch the bed of the sewing machine.

To prevent the fabric from slipping or loosening up while stitching, wrap the inner ring of the embroidery hoop with twill tape, or glue ¼" (6 mm) velvet ribbon to the outside edge of the inner ring (page 102). The inner ring will then grip the fabric, so it can be held more tightly in the hoop.

A spring-loaded hoop works very well for most decorative machine sewing. It holds the fabric securely without distorting the grainline or damaging the fabric. Always use a spring-loaded hoop for securing lightweight fabrics that can be easily damaged.

Stabilizers

Stabilizers are used for decorative stitching, to prevent puckering, stitch distortion, thread breakage, and skipped stitches. Stabilizers are especially helpful for appliqué, cutwork, machine embroidery, and monogramming.

Tear-away stabilizer is a nonwoven product that is either basted or pinned to the fabric; when pressed with an iron, some will temporarily adhere to the wrong side of the fabric. Tear-away stabilizer can easily be removed after the stitching is completed, by tearing it next to the stitches.

Water-soluble stabilizer is a translucent plastic film that is either basted or pinned to washable fabric. It is easily removed with water after the stitching is completed.

Tear-away stabilizer. Tear stabilizer close to stitches, taking care not to distort stitches. Use tweezers to remove any small pieces remaining under stitches.

Water-soluble stabilizer. Trim stabilizer close to stitches. To remove any remaining stabilizer, soak fabric in cool water for about five minutes, or spray stabilizer with cool water.

Sewing Machine Tension

Poor stitch quality detracts from the appearance of decorative stitches. Stabilizer is frequently used while sewing decorative stitches to help improve the quality of the stitches; stabilizer prevents puckering, stitch distortion, and skipped stitches. In addition to using stabilizer, you may need to adjust the tension of the machine to achieve perfect stitches.

In some types of decorative stitching, such as satin stitching and machine embroidery, the bobbin thread tends to show on the upper side of the fabric unless the tension is adjusted. A tension adjustment may also be necessary for decorative bobbin thread sewing (pages 34 and 35), because heavier specialty threads are used in the bobbin.

To check the tension, test-sew, using the same fabric, thread, and stitch type you will be using for the project. If you intend to use stabilizer when sewing the project, place the stabilizer under the fabric before sewing the test stitches. Start with regular tension on the machine; if regular tension does not give a good stitch, follow the instructions, below, for adjusting the machine tension.

Sequence for Adjusting the Tension for Specialty Bobbin Thread

1) Test-sew with specialty thread in the bobbin, using regular tension on the machine; some specialty threads work well without any adjustment.

2) Loosen needle thread tension, if regular tension does not give a good stitch. This allows heavier bobbin threads to lie on the surface of the fabric; heavier threads cannot penetrate fabric, unless the fabric is loosely woven.

3) Bypass the tension, according to the manual for your sewing machine, if adjusting the needle thread tension does not give a good stitch; heavier bobbin threads may feed more easily through the machine if the tension is bypassed. Follow the instructions, opposite, for bypassing the tension on wind-in-place bobbins.

4) Adjust the bobbin case tension screw, only as a last resort, according to the manual for your sewing machine. Do not attempt to adjust the tension screw if the manual does not include instructions.

How to Adjust the Tension for Satin Stitching and Machine Embroidery

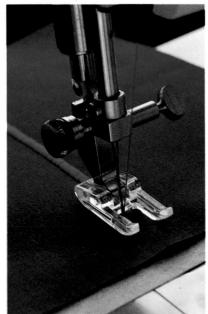

1) Thread machine with desired thread; set stitch width and stitch length. Place tear-away or water-soluble stabilizer under fabric scrap; stitch a row of satin stitching or machine embroidery.

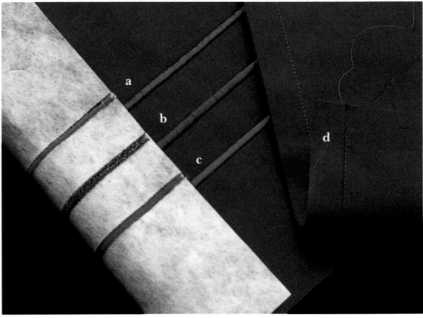

2) Check stitches. If bobbin thread shows on upper side **(a),** loosen needle thread tension. If needle thread is slack **(b),** tighten needle thread tension. Perfect tension on satin stitches and machine embroidery **(c)** does not cause puckering, and bobbin thread does not show on upper side; threads lock on underside of fabric. Perfectly balanced tension for regular sewing **(d)** does not cause puckering; threads draw equally into the fabric.

How to Bypass the Bobbin Thread Tension for Wind-in-place Bobbins

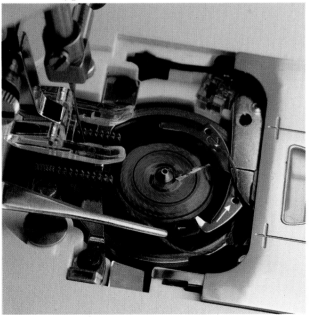

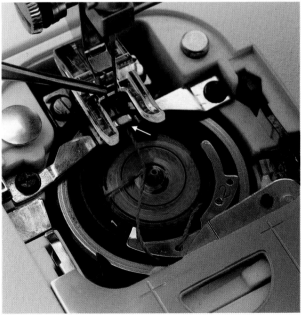

1) Wind bobbin by hand (page 35); insert bobbin. Remove needle plate. Bring bobbin thread through hole in bobbin case (arrow); for easier threading, apply liquid fray preventer to end of thread. Use tweezers to grasp end of thread.

2) Place bobbin thread under bobbin case retaining bridge (arrow). Replace needle plate, pulling bobbin thread through hole in plate. It may be necessary to loosen needle thread tension slightly to prevent thread from jamming.

Basic Stitches

Utility Stitch Patterns

The utility stitch patterns on a sewing machine were designed primarily to serve specific functions, such as blindstitching a hem or overcasting a seam; however, they can also be used as decorative stitching.

A twin needle can be used with utility stitches for a decorative look, following the guidelines in your manual for twin-needle stitching. You can also vary utility stitches by changing the stitch width or stitch length. Or change the look of the stitches by aligning or staggering the stitch patterns in two or more rows of stitching.

Straight stitch pattern can be stitched using a twin needle for two parallel rows of stitching in one step.

Zigzag stitch pattern or other utility stitch patterns can also be stitched using twin needle for an echo effect.

Fagoting stitch pattern can be varied by changing the stitch width and stitch length.

Multistitch-zigzag stitch pattern can be varied by changing the stitch length.

Blindstitch stitch pattern forms a new design when two rows of stitching are aligned opposite each other.

Overedge stitch pattern forms a new design when two rows of stitching are staggered.

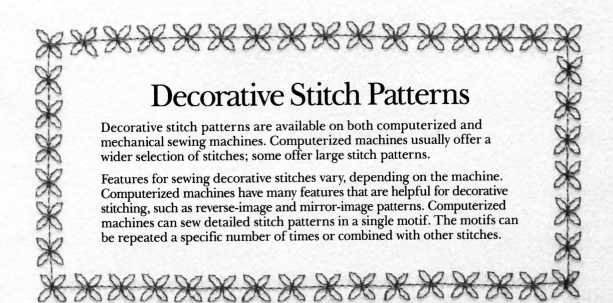

Decorative Stitch Patterns

Decorative stitch patterns are available on both computerized and mechanical sewing machines. Computerized machines usually offer a wider selection of stitches; some offer large stitch patterns.

Features for sewing decorative stitches vary, depending on the machine. Computerized machines have many features that are helpful for decorative stitching, such as reverse-image and mirror-image patterns. Computerized machines can sew detailed stitch patterns in a single motif. The motifs can be repeated a specific number of times or combined with other stitches.

Continuous stitch patterns can be used as border designs.

Single-motif stitch patterns can be stitched one motif at a time.

Large stitch patterns of 25 mm width are available on some computerized machines.

Reverse-image stitch patterns are alternated so motifs face outward in opposite directions.

Mirror-image stitch patterns are alternated so motifs face each other.

_A B C D E F G H I J_

Alphabet stitch pattern can be programmed to write words. Monograms, shown at right, are available on some computerized machines in various sizes and styles of lettering.

Using the Decorative Stitch Patterns

Accent a collar or cuffs with rows of decorative stitching. Mark placement lines and sew decorative stitches before assembling the collar or cuffs.

Decorative stitches can add just the right accent to a child's playsuit or an elegant blouse.

Deciding which of the many decorative stitches to use is the first step in planning a project. Whether you have a basic sewing machine with utility stitches or a top-of-the-line machine that also has automatic decorative stitches, there are several designs you can stitch (pages 22 and 23). On some machines, you can change the look of the stitches by varying the stitch length and stitch width.

Experiment with the stitches by sewing on fabric scraps, turning both left and right corners; some stitches may be attractive at both left and right corners, while others may look good only in one direction.

Also experiment with different types of thread. Changing from an all-purpose thread to a specialty thread, such as a shiny rayon, can change the effect of the stitching from sporty to dressy.

Sew the decorative stitches on the garment section before the seams are sewn, whenever possible, so the bulk of the seam allowances does not interfere with the stitching. It may be easier to sew the decorative stitches on the fabric before cutting out the garment piece.

Topstitch ribbed openings or hems of a T-shirt, using a utility stretch stitch instead of the straight stitch.

Make your own trim by sewing decorative stitches on a strip of contrasting fabric; then apply the trim with topstitching. You can also use rows of decorative stitching to add body to the brim of a hat.

Center a monogram on a turtleneck collar. Place tear-away stabilizer under the area to be monogrammed, to prevent the fabric from stretching.

Decorative Topstitching

Even the straight stitch can be decorative when it is used as topstitching. To make topstitching more noticeable, a heavier thread, such as topstitching thread or buttonhole twist, may be used in the needle; or use two strands of all-purpose thread. All-purpose thread is usually used in the bobbin.

Adjust the stitch length for topstitching according to the weight of the fabric. Short stitches are used on lightweight fabrics to prevent puckering, but longer stitches are more attractive on mediumweight to heavyweight fabrics. Check the stitch length and tension adjustments on a test sample, using the same thread, fabric, interfacing, and number of layers that you will use in the garment. Adjust the tension, if necessary, as on page 18.

To keep topstitching rows straight, it is helpful to use a guide, such as a blindstitch foot, quilting bar, or seam guide. A seam guide can also be made by placing layers of tape on the bed of the sewing machine. A thread tail can be used to guide fabric around corners without jamming.

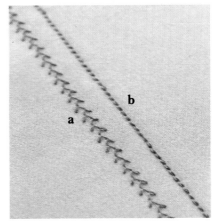

Feather stitch (a) can be set to a stitch width of 0 for the look of straight topstitching **(b).** The sewing machine sews back and forth three times, creating a heavier stitch.

Three Ways to Guide Topstitching

Use blindstitch or topstitching foot to guide edgestitching; place edge of fabric against presser foot guide.

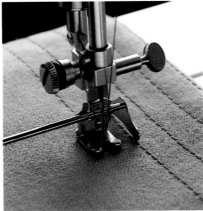

Use quilting bar to guide evenly spaced rows of topstitching; align the previous row with the end of quilting bar.

Make a seam guide for topstitching by building up a ridge on bed of machine with layers of tape.

How to Turn Corners

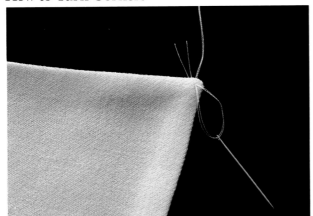

1) Take one stitch through corner of fabric, by hand or by machine, leaving long thread tails in fabric.

2) Topstitch to corner. Raise presser foot, leaving needle down in fabric; pivot. Lower presser foot, and hold onto thread tails as you continue to stitch.

Twin-needle Stitching

Twin-needle stitching is done using a twin needle, two needle threads, and a single bobbin thread. The bobbin thread draws the fabric up between the rows of stitching to form a decorative raised design or a pintuck. Twin-needle pintucks take up so little fabric that it is usually not necessary to allow extra fabric for the project.

Twin needles vary in size and are numbered according to the distance in millimeters between the needles and by the size of the needles. For example, a 2.0/80 twin needle has two size 80 needles, spaced 2 mm apart. When pintucks are sewn using twin needles, they are always even in width, because the two rows of stitching are exactly parallel.

A special-purpose presser foot or an open-toe foot is used for twin-needle stitching. A pintuck foot is used for sewing multiple rows of twin-needle pintucks. The grooves on the underside of the pintuck foot

keep the pintucks the same distance apart. Consult your sewing machine dealer about the pintuck feet available for your machine; there may be more than one size available to accommodate different weights of fabric. The narrower the grooves on the foot, the finer the pintucks will be. Use a larger-grooved foot for pintucks in bulkier fabrics. Choose the twin-needle size that most closely corresponds to the spacing of the grooves.

A more distinct raised appearance may be achieved in several ways. You can use a heavier thread in the bobbin to increase the tension on the underside. Or you can use cording to emphasize the raised design and to prevent puckering. Select the filler cord according to the size of the grooves in the pintuck foot. Buttonhole twist, pearl cotton, or gimp may be used. For a shadow effect on a sheer fabric, use a filler cord in a contrasting color.

How to Sew Multiple Rows of Twin-needle Pintucks

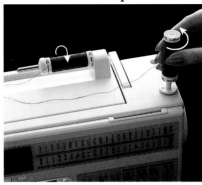

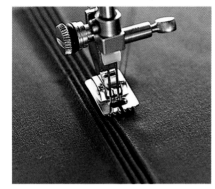

1) Place two spools of thread on machine so they unwind in opposite directions, to prevent tangling. Tighten needle thread tension, as necessary (page 18). Attach pintuck presser foot.

2) Mark placement line for first pintuck on right side of fabric. Stitch, guiding one needle along marked line.

3) Continue stitching rows, guiding previous tuck under one of the channels in pintuck foot; spacing between tucks depends on channel used. Stitch all pintucks in same direction to prevent distortion.

How to Sew Corded Twin-needle Stitching

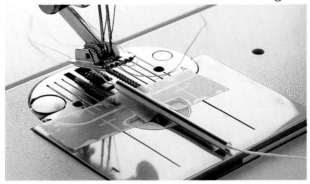

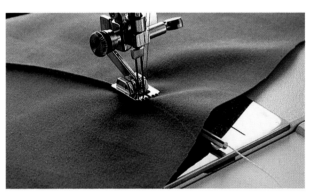

1) Thread machine and adjust tension as in step 1, above. Cut 2" (5 cm) length of drinking or cocktail straw. Tape straw to sewing machine bed directly in front of needle hole and ⅛" (3 mm) in front of presser foot. Thread end of cord through straw.

2) Place ball or spool of cord in lap. Stitch, placing cord under fabric and guiding fabric along marked design lines; cord automatically fills pintuck during stitching. For multiple rows of corded pintucks, use pintuck foot, and stitch as in step 3, above.

How to Turn Corners Using a Twin Needle

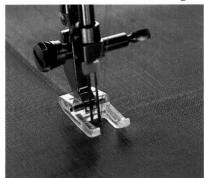

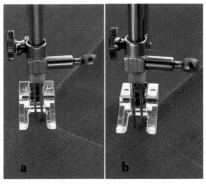

1) Thread machine and adjust the tension as in step 1, above. Using open-toe presser foot, stitch to corner; cord stitches, if desired, as above.

2) Raise presser foot, leaving needles down; turn fabric at a 45° angle, or halfway around corner **(a).** Lower presser foot. Take one stitch, turning flywheel by hand, taking care that inner needle stitches in place **(b).**

3) Leave needles down and raise presser foot. Turn fabric again to complete the corner. Lower the presser foot and continue stitching.

Satin Stitching

Satin stitching can be used to apply appliqués, outline cutwork, stitch decorative design lines, or finish edges.

To sew the satin stitch, set the machine for a zigzag stitch and a short stitch length, so the stitches lie close to each other, concealing all the fabric under the stitches. Satin stitches can be any stitch width desired; generally, the smaller the design, the narrower the stitch width.

Adjust the tension so the bobbin thread does not show on the upper side of the fabric (page 18). Use an open-toe presser foot or special-purpose presser foot for sewing satin stitching. The groove on the bottom of the foot provides space for the stitches, so the fabric feeds through the sewing machine evenly.

Machine embroidery thread is recommended for satin stitching (page 14). Cotton embroidery thread has a subtle sheen, rayon embroidery thread, a more pronounced sheen.

Satin stitching may be corded, using one to three strands of pearl cotton or topstitching thread . A cording foot is helpful, because it guides the cord under the stitches automatically. However, if a cording foot is not available for your sewing machine, the cord can be guided by hand.

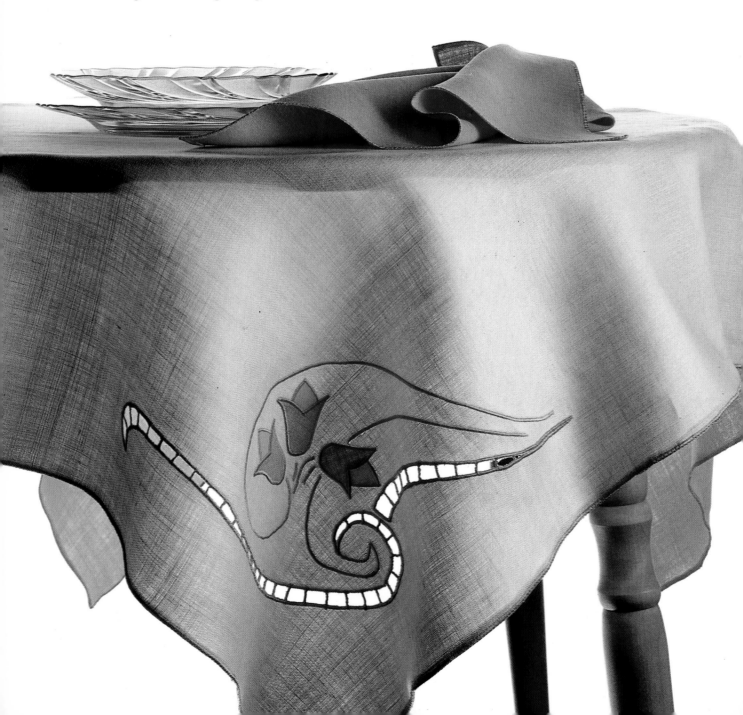

Setting the Stitch Length

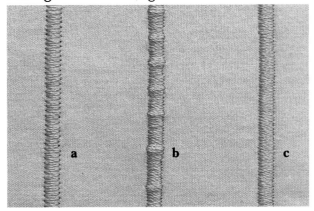

Set the stitch length for short stitches. Place a stabilizer under a fabric scrap, and stitch to check stitch length. If stitches are too long **(a),** the fabric shows between the stitches. If stitches are too short **(b),** the stitches pile up or overlap, and the fabric does not feed smoothly. Perfect satin stitches **(c)** are evenly spaced and lie next to each other without overlapping.

Two Ways to Sew an Edge Finish Using Satin Stitching

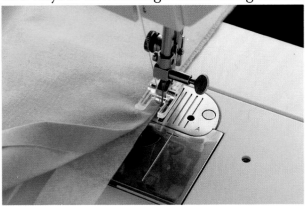

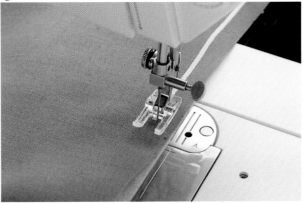

Folded edge. Press edge under ½" (1.3 cm). If using a lightweight fabric, place tear-away stabilizer under fabric, aligning it with fold. Stitch along folded edge so needle stitches just over fold. Turn corners or curves, as on pages 50 and 51. Remove stabilizer (page 17). Trim excess fabric close to stitches.

Single layer. Place 1" (2.5 cm) strip of tear-away or water-soluble stabilizer under edge. Satin stitch ½" (1.3 cm) from raw edge to prevent stretching at edge. Turn corners or curves, as on pages 50 and 51. Remove stabilizer (page 17). Trim fabric at edge, close to stitches.

How to Sew Corded Satin Stitching

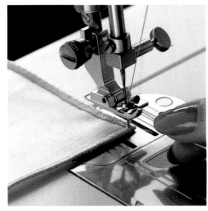

1) Satin stitch, above. Place pearl cotton in hole of cording foot. Stitch over cord along outer edge, using narrow zigzag stitch. Stop one stitch width away from corner, with needle down at inner edge; stitch in place for a few stitches.

2) Pivot fabric. Make a loop in cord and stitch in place for a few stitches. Continue zigzag stitching over cord for a few inches (2.5 cm). Pull on ends of cord to eliminate the loop.

3) Trim end of cord at starting point so cord ends meet. Overlap stitching ½" (1.3 cm).

Couching

Trims, such as pearl cotton, round cording, yarn, and braid, can be attached to a garment by couching over them with machine stitches. You can use specialty thread for decorative stitches or fine monofilament nylon thread for invisible stitches. To avoid flattening a rounded trim, select a stitch pattern on the machine that just catches the fabric on both sides of the trim, but does not pierce the trim itself.

If the design you are stitching has corners or tight curves, select a narrow, flexible trim. Wider trims can be couched successfully if the design has straight stitching lines or gradual curves.

Place tear-away stabilizer under the fabric during stitching to prevent puckering. If you are using a knit fabric or one that is lightweight or loosely woven, also apply fusible interfacing to the wrong side of the fabric before stitching.

It is helpful to use a cording foot for couching. The trim is threaded through the hole in the foot and is guided automatically, leaving your hands free to turn the fabric. The cording foot may also have a groove on the bottom, which allows narrow trims to feed smoothly. If a cording foot is not available, thread the trim through a piece of plastic tape applied to a presser foot, as shown opposite.

How to Couch Trims

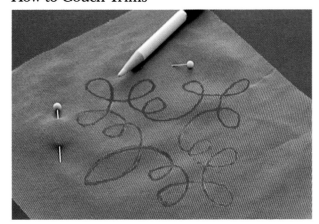

1) Trace design on nylon net. Position net over fabric; pin in place. Transfer design, using chalk or water-soluble marking pen.

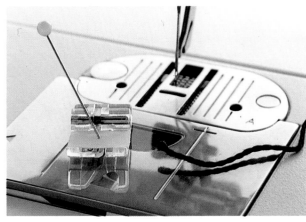

2) Place plastic tape on top of special-purpose or open-toe presser foot, if cording foot is not available. Puncture tape at center of needle hole opening in presser foot, making hole the width of trim.

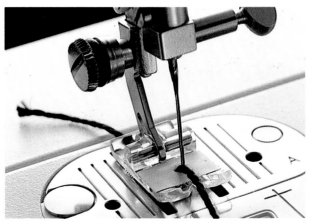

3) Place trim from front to back down through hole in tape, or through cording foot. Attach presser foot. Adjust stitch width so stitches will catch fabric on both sides of trim.

4) Place tear-away stabilizer under fabric in design area. Stitch over trim, guiding fabric so stitching follows marked line; trim feeds by itself.

5) Remove stabilizer (page 17). Brush away chalk markings or blot water-soluble markings with a damp cloth. Press fabric lightly on padded surface, from wrong side of fabric, taking care not to flatten trim.

How to Finish the Ends of Couched Trims

Thread end of trim through a tapestry needle and pull to the wrong side **(a)**; clip thread, leaving short tail. Or seal trimmed end with liquid fray preventer **(b).** Or enclose end in seamline **(c).**

Decorative Bobbin Thread Sewing

Specialty threads can be used to create many beautiful decorative effects. Threads that do not fit through the eye of a sewing machine needle can be used in the bobbin of the machine. Stitch with the fabric right side down, so the decorative thread shows on the right side of the fabric.

Heavy threads, such as pearl cotton, pearl rayon, metallic thread, six-strand embroidery floss, and ribbon thread, can be used for decorative bobbin thread sewing. Wind the threads on the bobbin, using one of the methods opposite.

Experiment to determine the types of specialty threads and decorative stitches that work best in your sewing machine. Test-sew on a fabric scrap, adjusting the stitch length and stitch width until you achieve the desired effect; adjust the tension of the machine, if necessary (pages 18 and 19). Check the stitches frequently on the underside of the fabric to ensure that the stitching is consistent.

Two Ways to Wind the Bobbin with Specialty Thread

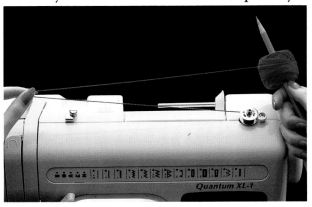

Wind bobbin slowly on the machine, leaving thread out of tension disc; control thread with hand, as necessary, to encourage even winding. If ball or cone does not fit on spool pin, place it over a pencil; hold pencil in hand while winding bobbin.

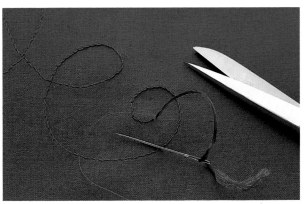

Wind bobbin evenly and firmly by hand, in same direction as it would be wound on the machine. This method can be used for all types of bobbins, but is always used for winding heavy threads on wind-in-place bobbins.

How to Sew with Decorative Bobbin Thread

1) Thread machine with all-purpose or lightweight monofilament nylon thread in needle. Wind bobbin with specialty thread, above. Attach open-toe presser foot. Test-sew, using regular tension. Adjust tension, if necessary (pages 18 and 19).

2) Mark design on tear-away or water-soluble stabilizer; if using an asymmetrical design, mark mirror image (pages 46 and 47). Baste or pin stabilizer to wrong side of fabric.

3) Stitch slowly, following design lines on stabilizer; hold needle and bobbin threads for the first few stitches to prevent jamming. Stitch continuously as much as possible; do not secure stitches at ends by backstitching or stitching in place.

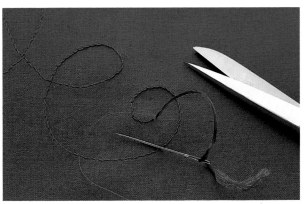

4) Remove stabilizer (page 17). Thread the end of bobbin thread through tapestry needle, and pull to wrong side. Knot thread ends; trim ends ½" (1.3 cm) from knots.

Appliqués

Appliqués

Appliqués can be the focal point of a garment; they can also be used for other projects, such as framed artwork, wall hangings, and tablecloths. Appliqués can be made from one fabric or from a combination of fabrics in various colors and textures. They can be bright and bold, or soft and subtle. Satin appliqués can add the perfect touch to an evening gown; velour appliqués can embellish a towel. You may sew a transparent appliqué on a negligee or one that is softly padded on a toddler's playsuit. The direction of the grainline can be varied on appliqué pieces for an interesting effect.

Select a background fabric that has enough body to support the weight of the appliqué and that will not stretch out of shape. Then check that the background fabric does not show through any light-colored fabrics in the appliqué. Appliqué fabrics can be interfaced with fusible knit interfacing, if necessary, to prevent show-through or to add body to the appliqué. The fusible knit interfacing will not cause the appliqué to become stiff.

Garments can be dressed up with appliqués made from silky fabrics.

Appliqués can be creatively embellished with ribbons or other trims for added dimension.

Home decorating projects, such as curtains, can be enhanced with appliqués to complement any decorating scheme.

Appliqués are stitched to the garment using satin stitching. The width of the stitches depends on the size of the appliqué; use wider stitches for larger appliqués. Machine embroidery thread (page 14) is recommended for satin stitching, but all-purpose thread, which is available in a wider color selection, may be used. After threading the machine, adjust the tension (page 18) so the bobbin threads do not show on the right side of the fabric. The color of the thread may be changed, as desired, to blend or contrast with different areas of the appliqué.

There are several ways to apply an appliqué (pages 44 and 45), depending on the fabrics used and the effect you want to create. Tear-away stabilizer is used on the wrong side of the background fabric to prevent the stitches from puckering.

Appliquéd garments may be washed and dried by machine if the fabrics are washable. To prevent excessive abrasion of the appliqué, turn the garment wrong side out before washing.

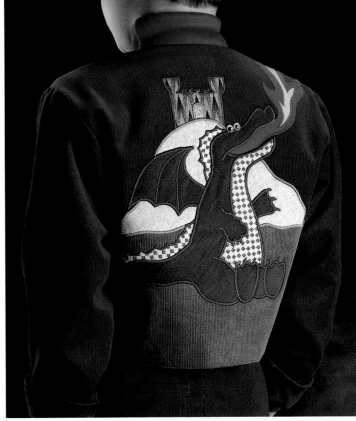

Children's clothing can be brightened with a whimsical appliqué.

Dinnerware designs can be copied and used for appliqués on table linens.

Designing Appliqués

Many designs can be adapted for appliqués. If the design is smaller or larger than you want, it can be enlarged or reduced, using a photocopy machine. Elaborate or detailed designs can be simplified to make the appliqué easier to sew.

Artwork, stencils, greeting cards, and children's drawings can be good sources of inspiration for appliqués. Or you may want to draw your own appliqué design; geometric designs are easy to draw and make interesting appliqué shapes that are also easy to sew.

When designing an appliqué, decide on the size and basic shape of the area you want to cover. Keep in mind that appliqués do not show up as well on areas of the garment that curve around the body.

Select a garment pattern that will work with the appliqué design you have chosen. It is usually best to select a pattern that has simple design lines, so the appliqué will be the center of interest on the garment.

Greeting cards frequently have simple artwork to use as inspiration for appliqué designs.

Paintings and other forms of artwork can inspire an appliqué design. Simplify the shapes, because appliqués are easier to cut and stitch if they are not intricate.

Books, such as pictorial design books and children's coloring books, offer a wide selection of appliqué ideas.

Positioning the Appliqué

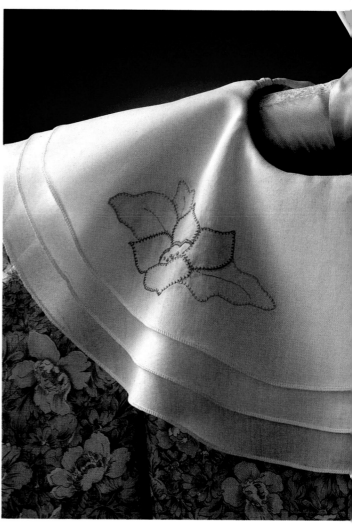

Appliqués can be used to add interest to nearly any section of a garment. For example, they can encircle a neckline or a hemline, accent one or both shoulders, or embellish the front and back of a garment.

To mark the placement of an appliqué, baste the seams of the garment so it can be tried on. If the appliqué will be positioned over a seamline, permanently stitch and press that seam. Try on the garment and position the appliqué, to ensure that the placement of the design is appropriate. Appliqués may wrap around the sides of a garment, but the focal point of an appliqué is usually positioned in the front or back, where it is most noticeable.

For vertical placement of an appliqué, mark a vertical center line on the appliqué and align it to the grainline of the garment. For centered symmetrical designs, align the center line of the appliqué to the center line of the garment.

Designs that are asymmetrical are frequently positioned to one side of the project.

How to Mark the Placement of an Appliqué

1) Baste seams; stitch any seams that will be under appliqué, using regular stitch length. Place pattern for appliqué design in desired position. Pin in place, using safety pins.

2) Remove basting so project lies flat. Place on cutting board or padded surface. Insert straight pins with small heads, straight down through pattern and fabric, marking placement points of appliqué.

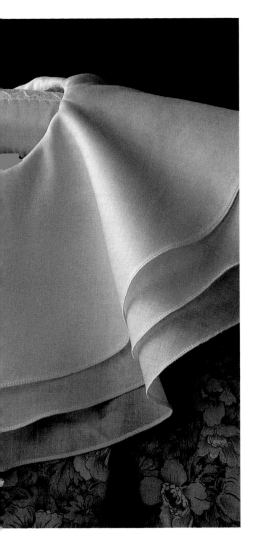

Designs that are symmetrical usually look best when they are centered on the project.

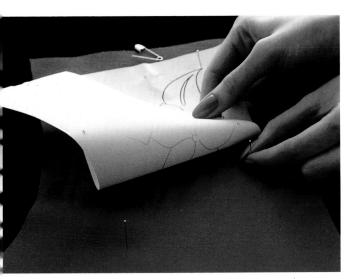

3) Remove safety pins, and carefully lift pattern, leaving straight pins in fabric.

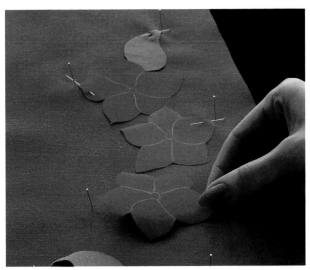

4) Position appliqué on project, matching appliqué to placement points.

Selecting an Appliqué Technique

There are several ways to apply appliqués. The method you select depends on the look you want to create, the fabrics you are using, and whether you want a supple appliqué or one with more body.

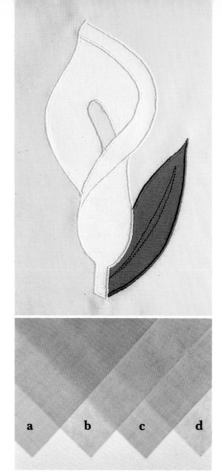

Fused Appliqués

The appliqué fabric (a) is cut to shape and secured with fusible web (b) to the background fabric (c). Tear-away stabilizer (d) is placed under the background fabric; then satin stitching is done from the right side to cover the raw edges.

Considerations

Fusible web causes appliqué to become somewhat stiff.

Appliqué cannot shift or ripple during stitching, because it is fused to the background fabric.

Use basic fabrics, such as cotton broadcloth, poplin, or other lightweight to mediumweight fabrics that fuse securely.

Avoid using fabrics that will become too stiff when fusible web is applied, such as chintz, or those that will bubble when fused, such as some silky fabrics.

Reverse Appliqués

The appliqué fabric (a) is placed on the right side of the background fabric (b); the appliqué shape is not cut out. The design is marked on tear-away stabilizer (c) and the stabilizer is placed on the wrong side of the background fabric.

The design lines are stitched from the wrong side, using straight stitching. Then the appliqué fabric is trimmed close to the stitching, and satin stitching is done from the right side to cover the raw edges.

Considerations

Appliqué is supple, because fusible web is not used.

Appliqué fabric is secured to the background fabric by straight stitching from the wrong side of the project before cutting it to the shape of the design.

Use this method for satins and other fabrics that do not fuse well with fusible web. Use a hoop, if necessary, to keep silky fabrics smooth.

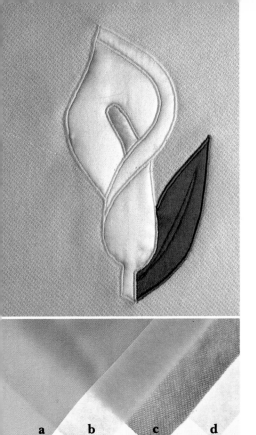

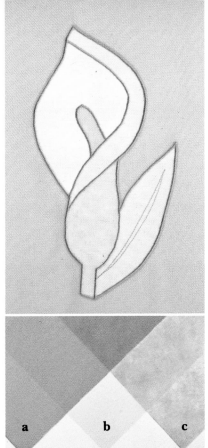

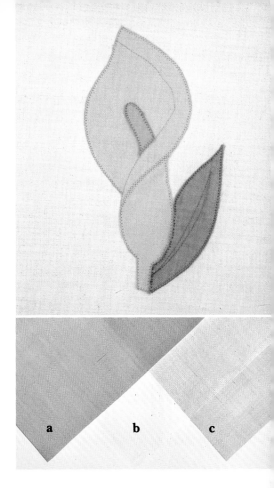

Padded Appliqués

The appliqué fabric (**a**) is placed over layers of polyester fleece or quilt batting (**b**) and background fabric (**c**); the appliqué shape is not cut out. The design is marked on tear-away stabilizer (**d**) and the stabilizer is placed on the wrong side of the background fabric.

The design lines are stitched from the wrong side, using straight stitching. Then the appliqué fabric and fleece are trimmed close to the stitching, and satin stitching is done from the right side to cover the raw edges.

Considerations

Appliqué fabric and fleece are secured to the background fabric by straight stitching from the wrong side of the project before cutting them to the shape of the design.

Use lightweight to mediumweight appliqué fabrics. Because the polyester fleece or quilt batting adds bulk to the appliqué, avoid using bulky or stiff appliqué fabrics. Heavier background fabrics may be used with padded appliqués.

Transparent Appliqués

The appliqué fabrics (**a**) are layered under the background fabric (**b**); the appliqué shapes are not cut out. The design is marked on tear-away stabilizer (**c**) and the stabilizer is then placed on the wrong side of the appliqué fabric.

The design lines are stitched from the wrong side, using straight stitching. Then one or more layers of fabric are trimmed from the right side close to the stitching to make transparent openings. Satin stitching is done from the right side to cover the raw edges.

Considerations

Appliqué is transparent in some areas of the design.

Multiple layers of sheer fabric give a more opaque appearance.

Several sheer or opaque fabrics can be used, including chiffon, sheer tricot, organza, and organdy.

Shadow Appliqués

The design is marked on the garment fabric (**a**). Water-soluble stabilizer (**b**) is placed under the garment fabric. The appliqué fabric (**c**) is placed under the stabilizer; the appliqué shape is not cut out.

The design lines are stitched from the right side, using decorative stitching. Then the appliqué fabric is trimmed close to the stitching.

Considerations

Appliqué is supple because no fusible web or interfacing is used.

Lightweight appliqué fabrics are layered under sheer or lightweight garment fabric, creating a shadow effect.

Several sheer or opaque fabrics can be used, including Swiss cotton, batiste, organdy, and lightweight broadcloth. Avoid using fabrics that ravel easily. Use washable fabric, because water-soluble stabilizer is used.

Fused Appliqués

Fused appliqués are the easiest to apply, because they are secured to the project with paper-backed fusible web. Although the fusible web adds some stiffness, it prevents the appliqué from shifting or rippling during stitching. Using this technique, it is possible to make appliqués in intricately shaped designs.

Fused appliqués work best with basic fabrics, such as cotton broadcloth or poplin, because they fuse well. Knit fabrics may also be used; apply fusible knit interfacing to knit fabrics to stabilize them before applying the fusible web. Sheer or light-colored fabrics should also be interfaced with fusible knit interfacing, to prevent background fabric from showing through the appliqué. Avoid using fabrics that bubble when fusible web is applied, such as some satin fabrics.

The appliqué is marked on the paper backing of the fusible web before it is applied. Because the fusible web is applied to the wrong side of the fabric, it is necessary to trace the mirror image of any asymmetrical appliqué design to prevent it from being reversed on the right side of the garment. To do this, hold the pattern up to a light source. A light table is helpful for tracing patterns; if you do not have a light table, a temporary one can be made by placing a light under a glass-top table. Or you can hold the pattern up to a window during daylight hours.

How to Sew an Appliqué Using Paper-backed Fusible Web

1) Hold the appliqué pattern up to a light if using an asymmetrical design, and trace the mirror image of the design onto back of pattern.

2) Use mirror image of design to trace pieces of the appliqué onto paper side of paper-backed fusible web, using lead pencil; add ¼" (6 mm) to sides of any pieces that will underlap another piece.

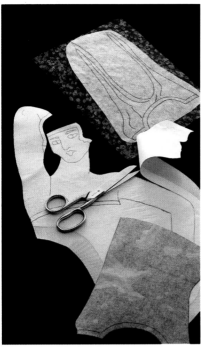

3) Cut around design, leaving a margin. Place the fusible web on the wrong side of appliqué fabric, with paper backing up. Press with a hot, dry iron for a few seconds. Allow fabric to cool. Cut out the appliqué pieces.

4) Transfer any additional design lines to the *right* side of fabric by holding appliqué piece up to light. Remove paper from paper-backed fusible web.

5) Mark placement of appliqué on garment (pages 42 and 43). Position appliqué pieces; fuse to right side of garment following manufacturer's directions.

6) Cut tear-away stabilizer at least 2" (5 cm) larger than the appliqué. Place stabilizer under the appliqué area on wrong side of garment; pin in place from right side.

(Continued on next page)

How to Sew an Appliqué Using Paper-backed Fusible Web (continued)

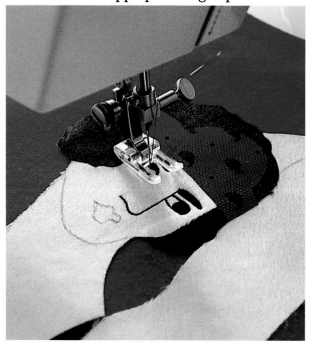

7) Set machine for short, straight stitches. Stitch on marked lines, outlining any fine design details, such as facial features. Fill in design areas, as desired, by stitching several rows close together.

8) Set machine for closely spaced zigzag stitches; set stitch width, as desired. Loosen needle thread tension, if necessary, so bobbin thread will not show on right side of fabric. Satin stitch around appliqué and any remaining design lines (pages 50 and 51). Remove tear-away stabilizer (page 17).

How to Sew a Gathered Appliqué Using Fusible Web

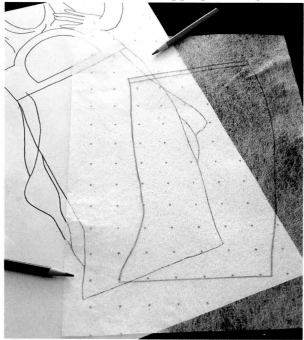

1) Place tissue paper over mirror-image side of the appliqué pattern; tape or pin in place. Trace outline of appliqué piece to be gathered; add ¼" (6 mm) seam allowance on edge to be gathered. Remove tissue.

2) Slash tissue pattern at several places, from edge to be gathered to, but not through, opposite edge. Place paper under tissue pattern. Spread tissue on slashed lines so edge to be gathered measures 1¼ times original length; tape in place.

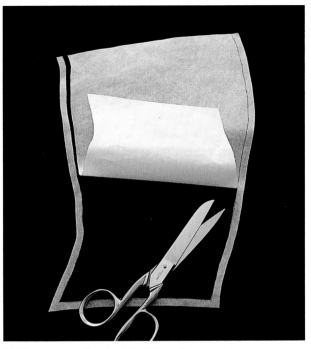

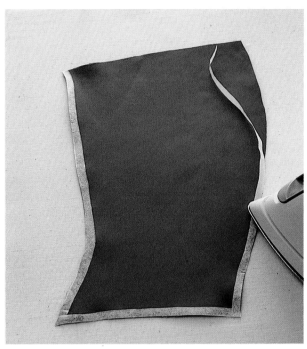

3) Place paper-backed fusible web over tissue pattern; trace outline. Draw lines ¼" (6 mm) inside traced outline on sides that will not be gathered; cut fusible web on marked lines to make ¼" (6 mm) strip.

4) Place tissue pattern on wrong side of fabric; cut appliqué piece. Place fusible web on wrong side of appliqué, with paper backing up; press with hot, dry iron for a few seconds. Allow fabric to cool.

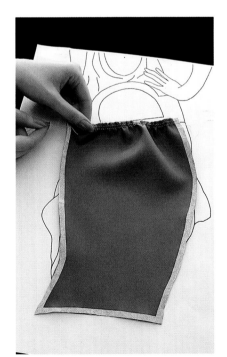

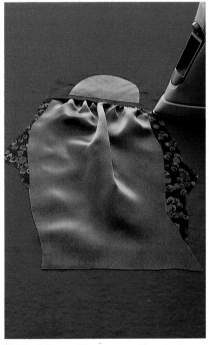

5) Stitch two rows of gathering stitches on side of appliqué to be gathered. Pull up gathers to original length of appliqué pattern. Remove paper backing from fusible web.

6) Mark placement on garment (pages 42 and 43). Fuse piece to garment, following manufacturer's directions. Straight-stitch gathered side in place ¼" (6 mm) from edge. Trim close to stitching.

7) Position adjacent appliqué piece so edge overlaps the gathered piece up to the stitching line; fuse. Fuse any remaining appliqué pieces, and complete appliqué (pages 47 and 48, steps 6 to 8).

How to Satin Stitch Corners and Curves of Appliqués

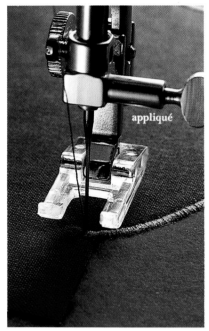

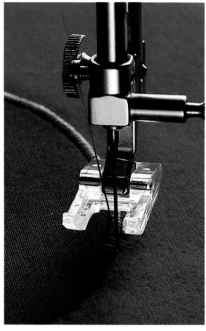

Inside corners. Stitch past corner a distance equal to width of satin stitch, stopping with needle down at the inner edge of satin stitching; raise presser foot. Pivot and satin stitch next side of appliqué, covering previous stitches at corner.

Outside corners. Stitch one stitch past corner, stopping with needle down at outer edge of satin stitching; raise presser foot. Pivot and satin stitch the next side of appliqué, covering previous stitches at corner.

Curves. Pivot fabric frequently, pivoting with needle down at longest edge of satin stitching.

How to Satin Stitch Outside Points of Appliqués

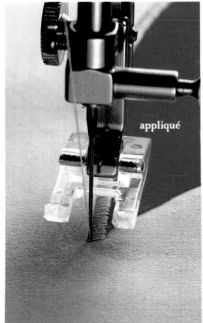

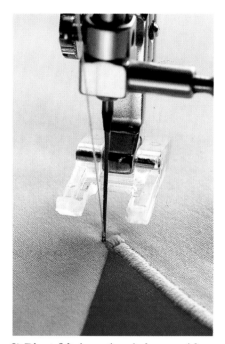

1) Stitch one stitch past the point, stopping with needle down at outer edge of satin stitching; raise the presser foot.

2) Pivot fabric to a 90° angle. Stitch two to four stitches, stopping when stitches just cover previous stitches; stop with needle down on outer edge of satin stitching. Raise the presser foot.

3) Pivot fabric; satin stitch next side of appliqué.

How to Satin Stitch Inside Points of Appliqués

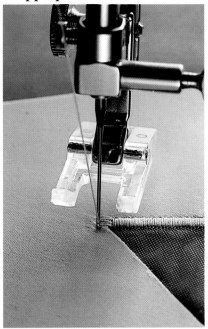

1) Stitch past the point a distance equal to the width of satin stitch, stopping with needle down at inner edge of the satin stitching; raise the presser foot.

2) Pivot fabric to a 90° angle. Stitch two to four stitches, stopping when stitches just cover previous stitches; stop with needle down on inner edge of satin stitching. Raise presser foot.

3) Pivot fabric; satin stitch next side of appliqué.

How to Satin Stitch Tapered Outside Points of Appliqués

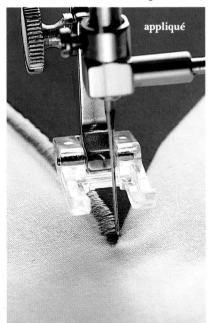

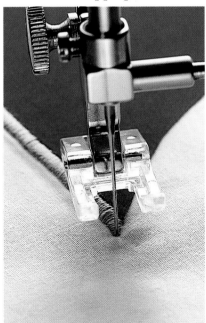

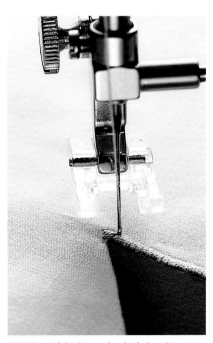

1) Stitch, stopping when inner edge of satin stitching meets other side of appliqué. Raise presser foot.

2) Pivot fabric slightly. Continue stitching, gradually narrowing stitch width to 0 and stopping at point. Raise presser foot.

3) Pivot fabric and stitch back over the previous stitches, gradually widening stitch width to original width. Pivot fabric slightly and stitch next side of appliqué.

Reverse Appliqués

Reverse appliqués are used when you want a supple appliqué, because they are not stiffened with fusible web. The appliqué shapes are not cut until after the outline of the design is stitched to the background fabric. When sewing appliqués from satin, challis, or other fabrics that are either silky or lack body, it may be necessary to secure the fabric layers in an embroidery hoop to prevent rippling while the

design outline is being stitched. The appliqué design is marked on tear-away stabilizer, and the stabilizer is placed on the wrong side of the fabric; because of this, it is necessary to trace the mirror image of any asymmetrical appliqué design to prevent it from being reversed on the right side of the garment (pages 46 and 47).

How to Apply a Reverse Appliqué

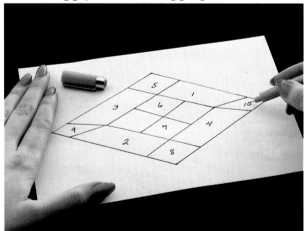

1) Decide sequence for stitching the appliqué pieces, starting with those that should appear to be under other pieces; number areas in sequence of stitching.

2) Cut tear-away stabilizer at least 2" (5 cm) larger than entire design area. Trace design onto stabilizer; if using an asymmetrical design, trace mirror image (pages 46 and 47).

3) Mark placement of appliqué on garment, as on pages 42 and 43, steps 1 to 3. Position stabilizer on wrong side of garment, matching placement points of design to pins. Pin or baste stabilizer to garment.

4) Cut fabric larger than first piece to be appliquéd; do not cut out appliqué shape. Place appliqué fabric, right side up, on right side of garment. Baste or pin; if pins are used, place pins on wrong side of garment.

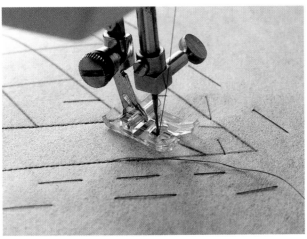

5) Stitch on design lines from wrong side, using straight stitches. Outline and fill in fine details, such as facial features, if any, as on page 48, step 7.

6) Remove basting or pins used in step 4. Trim excess appliqué fabric close to stitching from right side.

7) Repeat steps 4 to 6 for each piece in appliqué, applying pieces in sequence.

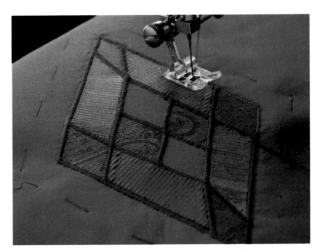

8) Set machine for closely spaced zigzag stitches; set stitch width as desired. Loosen needle thread tension, if necessary, so bobbin thread will not show on right side. Satin stitch on design lines. Remove stabilizer.

Padded Appliqués

A softly padded effect can be achieved
by placing low-loft quilt batting or polyester
fleece under the appliqué fabric. A padded
appliqué is stitched from the wrong side before
cutting the appliqué fabric and batting to the shape
of the design. This eliminates any concern about keeping
the layers even at the edges of the appliqué during stitching
and is especially helpful if you are sewing an appliqué from
lightweight or silky fabrics. If necessary, fabrics can be secured in an
embroidery hoop to prevent rippling while the design outline is stitched.

How to Apply a Padded Appliqué

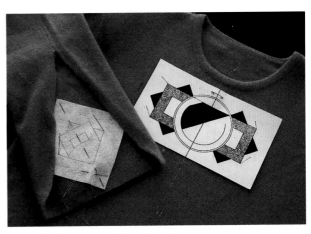

1) Cut tear-away stabilizer at least 2" (5 cm) larger than entire area to be appliquéd. Trace design onto stabilizer; if using an asymmetrical design, trace the mirror image (pages 46 and 47).

2) Mark placement of appliqué on garment, as on pages 42 and 43, steps 1 to 3. Position stabilizer on wrong side of garment, matching placement points of design to pins. Baste or pin stabilizer to garment.

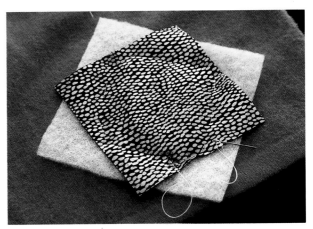

3) Cut piece of low-loft quilt batting or polyester fleece larger than entire area to be appliquéd; place on right side of garment over design area.

4) Cut fabric for appliqué piece larger than design area; do not cut out appliqué shape. Place appliqué fabric, right side up, over fleece. Baste or pin; if pins are used, place pins on wrong side of garment.

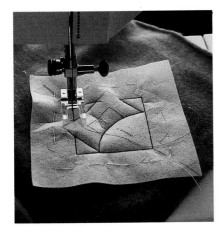

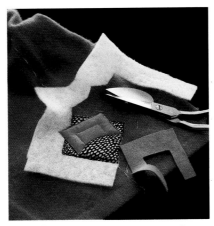

5) Stitch design lines on stabilizer, using short, straight stitches. Remove basting or pins used in step 4. Trim excess appliqué fabric close to the stitching from right side.

6) Repeat steps 4 and 5 for each appliqué piece. Trim fleece close to stitching.

7) Satin stitch from right side, as on page 48, step 8. Remove the stabilizer (page 17).

Transparent Appliqués

One or more layers of sheer fabric can be used to make an elegant transparent appliqué. The sheer fabric is placed on the wrong side of the background fabric; the layers are stitched together along the design lines, and the background fabric is trimmed away from the right side to create sheer openings.

If several layers of sheer fabric are used, you can trim just one or two layers in some of the design areas for an opaque effect and trim all but one layer in other areas for a more transparent effect.

How to Apply a Transparent Appliqué

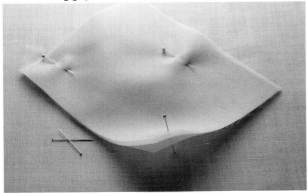

1) Mark placement of appliqué, as on pages 42 and 43, steps 1 to 3. Place background fabric right side down. Pin one or more layers of sheer fabric to background fabric, right side down, inserting pins at placement points of design. Remove pins from right side of fabric.

2) Cut tear-away stabilizer at least 2" (5 cm) larger than area to be appliquéd. Trace design onto stabilizer; if using an asymmetrical design, trace the mirror image (pages 46 and 47). Position stabilizer over sheer fabric layers, matching placement points of design; pin in place. Baste stabilizer to garment through all layers. Remove pins.

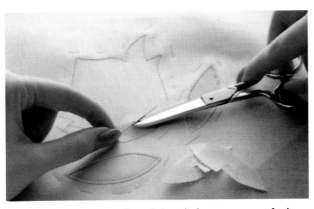

3) Stitch three rows of straight stitches on outer design lines from wrong side, using short stitch length. Trim background fabric within design areas close to stitching. Insert a pin into background fabric layer; lift and clip a few threads, making an opening that allows for easier trimming without cutting sheer fabric.

4) Stitch three rows of straight stitches on remaining design lines, from wrong side. Trim away one or more sheer layers from right side of fabric, within design areas, using a pin to separate sheer layers for easier trimming.

5) Set machine for closely spaced zigzag stitches; set stitch width, as desired. Loosen needle thread tension, if necessary, so bobbin thread will not show on right side. Satin stitch around appliqué, as for cutwork (pages 74 and 75).

6) Remove tear-away stabilizer (page 17). Trim excess sheer fabric outside design area, from wrong side, close to the stitching.

Shadow Appliqués

Shadow appliqué is a machine-stitched technique resembling shadow work embroidery. Lightweight appliqué fabrics are layered under a lightweight or sheer garment fabric, creating a shadow effect.

Batiste and broadcloth work well for appliqué fabrics. Select a garment fabric that is sheer enough to allow the color of the appliqué to show through, such as Swiss cotton, batiste, organdy, or handkerchief linen. Avoid using fabrics that ravel easily. It is important to preshrink fabrics before sewing, especially if using several types of fabric, because different fibers may shrink differently.

Select fabric and thread colors carefully, checking the colors, as shown at right, to see the actual effect of the fabrics and threads in the finished project. If the garment is to be lined, also check the color of the lining fabric. Appliqué and lining fabrics will appear to be somewhat lighter in color after they are layered,

depending on how sheer the garment fabric is. Select thread colors that are the same as or slightly darker than the colors of the appliqué fabrics.

Use a fine 60-weight cotton machine embroidery thread or a 40-weight rayon thread in the needle of the machine. Use a fine 60-weight cotton machine embroidery thread in the bobbin.

Use a sharp, new size 70/9 sewing machine needle when sewing shadow appliqués, because lightweight fabrics and fine threads are used.

Select decorative machine stitches, shown at right, that will highlight the design without overpowering it. The settings for stitch width and stitch length will vary, depending on the stitch pattern you select and the size of the appliqué piece.

It is important that you practice shadow appliqué techniques before beginning a project. Use the

Selecting Fabric and Thread Colors

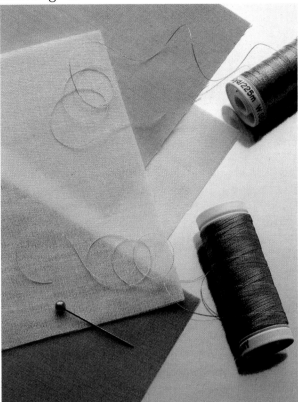

Layer small swatches of appliqué fabrics under the garment fabric to see how colors will appear when applied. For lined garments, check lining color by placing it under appliqué swatches. Check each thread color to be used by placing one strand of thread on layered appliqué fabric.

Selecting Decorative Stitches

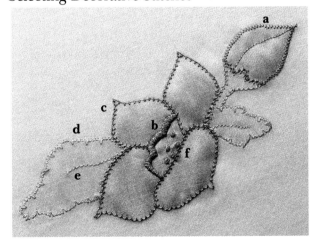

Select decorative stitches that highlight the design without overpowering it, such as zigzag (**a**), satin (**b**), blanket (**c**), and blindstitch (**d**). The straight stitch (**e**) can be used to stitch design details within the appliqué areas; do not use it for the outer edges of appliqué pieces, because it does not secure appliqués well and fabric will ravel. Machine-stitched French knots (**f**) can also be used.

selected fabrics and threads, to become familiar with the techniques and to check the selection of stitches, fabrics, and threads.

Apply spray starch to the right side of the garment fabric; then trace the design on the right side, using a slightly dull No. 2 lead pencil. Pencil marks will wash out easily with mild soap if spray starch has been applied to the fabric.

Place water-soluble stabilizer under the appliqué area and place the layered fabrics in a 5" to 7" (12.5 to 18 cm) embroidery hoop. Spring-loaded hoops are recommended for securing the lightweight fabrics, because they hold the fabrics taut without distorting the grainline and damaging the fabrics.

When pressing shadow appliqués, place the appliqué face down on two or three layers of velour towels and press the appliqué from the wrong side. The padded surface prevents the stitching from being flattened.

How to Apply a Shadow Appliqué

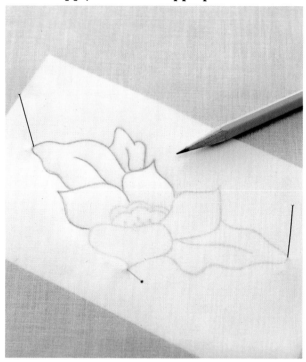

1) Starch garment fabric on right side in design area, using spray starch; press. Mark placement of the appliqué on garment, as on pages 42 and 43, steps 1 to 3. Position pattern for appliqué on wrong side of fabric; match placement points of design to pins. Trace design on right side of fabric, using dull No. 2 pencil.

2) Cut water-soluble stabilizer larger than embroidery hoop. Place stabilizer on wrong side of fabric.

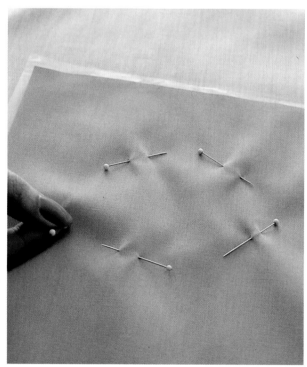

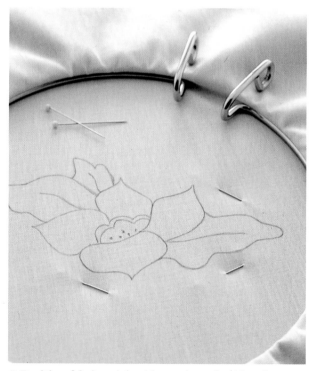

3) Cut appliqué fabric larger than entire design area for the fabric color. Place appliqué fabric, right side down, on stabilizer; pin.

4) Position fabrics, right side up, in embroidery hoop (page 103). Remove pins, or repin fabric from right side if appliqué fabric is not secured in hoop.

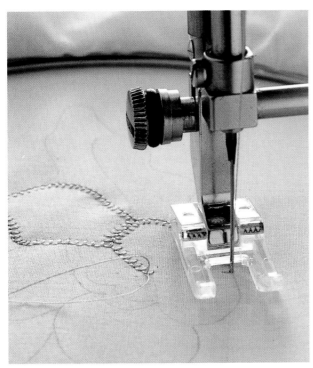

5) Set straight stitch length for 20 to 25 stitches per inch (2.5 cm). Draw up bobbin thread on design line; do not start at a corner. Stitch in place a few times to secure stitches. Stitch along outer design lines, using decorative stitches, so right swing of needle is on the line and left swing of needle is within design area. Stitch corners, curves, and dividing lines, as on page 63.

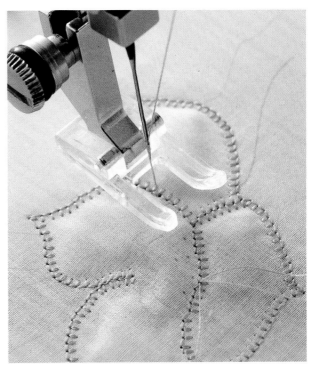

6) Stitch in place a few times at end of design area, to secure stitches. Raise presser foot and pull threads to next design area of same fabric color. Stitch all designs for same fabric color, securing threads at beginning and end of stitching. Clip thread tails.

7) Trim excess appliqué fabric close to stitching from the wrong side.

8) Repeat steps 3 to 7 for each appliqué fabric color, changing thread color and decorative stitch pattern, as desired.

(Continued on next page)

9) Set machine for straight stitches of 14 to 16 stitches per inch (2.5 cm) to sew outline stitching. Stitch on design lines in center areas of appliqués. Stitch French knots, opposite, if included in design.

10) Satin stitch areas as desired, with closely spaced zigzag stitches. Draw up bobbin thread; stitch in place a few times to secure stitches. Starting with stitch width at 0, gradually widen stitch width as you sew, following shape of area. Taper the stitching, as necessary, by narrowing stitch width.

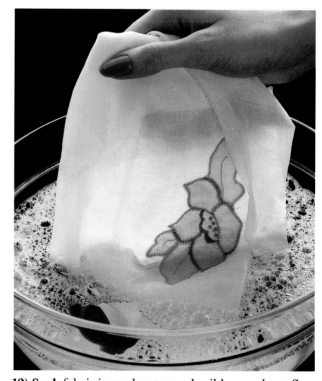

11) Trim excess water-soluble stabilizer around the appliqué design.

12) Soak fabric in cool water and mild soap about five minutes to remove the stabilizer between fabric layers, and the pencil markings.

How to Stitch Corners, Curves, and Dividing Lines of Shadow Appliqués

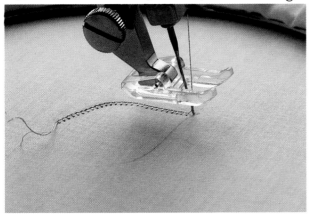

Corners. 1) Stitch to corner, stopping with needle down at right swing of stitch; it may be necessary to turn corner, slightly before or beyond marked design line. Raise presser foot.

2) Turn hoop to pivot; the first stitch around corner (arrow) is stitched inside the design area. Pivot and stitch next side of appliqué.

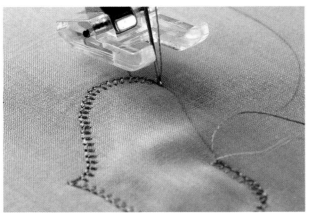

Curves. Pivot fabric frequently, with needle down on design line, turning hoop slightly; stitches should point to center of design.

Dividing lines. Butt stitches together where two areas of design share a common design line; align stitches so they meet directly opposite each other.

How to Make Machine-stitched French Knots

1) Cover feed dogs with cover plate or lower them. Draw up bobbin thread. Stitch in place a few times to secure stitches; clip thread tails. Set machine for zigzag stitches, setting stitch width according to size of French knot desired. Stitch 10 complete zigzag stitches, or until threads begin to round over sides, forming a ball.

2) Set machine for straight stitches. Take two stitches in center of knot **(a)**. Raise presser foot. Take one stitch in front of knot, close to ball of thread **(b)**. Take two stitches in center of knot again, to secure threads **(a)**. Pull gently on tail; clip threads close to stitching.

Piecing the Background Fabric

To create an overall effect for an appliquéd project, the background may be pieced, providing a setting or backdrop for the appliqué. For example, you can create a landscape effect if the lower portion of the garment is green and the upper portion, blue. Or add textural interest to a project by using a combination of smooth and textured fabrics for the background.

The background is pieced before the appliqué is applied. To plan the placement of the design, draw the background and appliqué design lines on a full-size pattern piece. If sewing a garment, pin-fit the pattern to check the placement lines for the background fabrics; the exact position of the appliqué itself can be planned after the main garment seams are basted (pages 42 and 43).

Stitch the design lines on the background fabric, using satin stitches, to match the stitching on the appliqué.

How to Piece the Background of the Appliqué

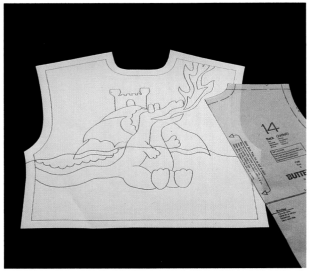

1) Make a full-size pattern piece for the garment section. Draw appliqué design, including background design lines, on pattern. Pin-fit the pattern to check placement of design lines for background fabric.

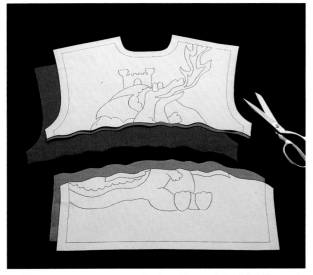

2) Cut pattern apart on design lines. Add ¼" (6 mm) seam allowance for underlap to one pattern piece at design line, using tissue paper. Cut garment pieces from fabric.

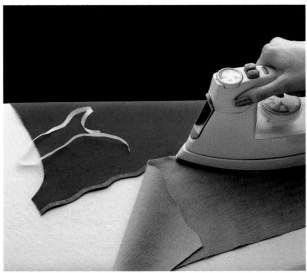

3) Cut paper-backed fusible web to size and shape of seam allowance; fuse in place on underlap of garment piece. Remove paper backing from fusible web. Overlap adjoining garment piece; fuse.

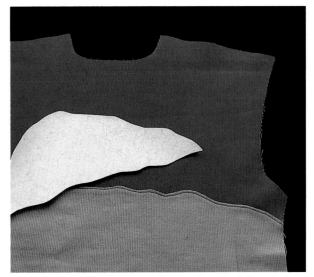

4) Stitch close to the raw edge, using straight stitch. Apply appliqué; satin stitch over the raw edge of the background when satin stitching appliqué (pages 50 and 51).

Embellishing Appliqués

To add interest and dimension to an appliqué design, appliqués can be embellished with trims. For example, a pom-pom can be used as a decorative nose for a clown or teddy bear, a buckle can be added to an appliquéd belt, or ribbons can be tied to the string of an appliquéd kite.

The fabrics used in the appliqué can be embellished with decorative machine stitches. Or hemstitching, machine embroidery, and cutwork can be used to embellish some pieces of an appliqué.

Ribbons or cords can be tacked in place or inserted under edge of appliqué before satin stitching to secure them.

Notions, such as pearls, pom-poms, or bells, can be stitched on appliqués or glued in place with permanent fabric glue.

Decorative stitching can embellish some of the appliqué pieces and add detail to the appliqué.

Movable eyes can be stitched or glued in place. Buttons can also be used for eyes.

Heirloom Sewing

Pintucks are formed by stitching very near a folded edge or by topstitching with a twin needle and a pintuck foot.

Heirloom sewing is a catchall term for the techniques that seamstresses in the Victorian era used to embellish plain fabrics, because they did not have the wide selection of printed and textured fabrics that are available today.

Originally, these techniques required many hours of painstaking hand sewing. But, with the conventional sewing machine, home sewers can create similar looks in a fraction of the time.

Heirloom techniques look best when sewn in woven fabrics of natural fibers or in blends consisting mostly of natural fibers. Some of the techniques in this section can be successfully sewn in many types of fabrics, but the heirloom appearance may be lost when knits or synthetic silkies are used. Specific fabric suggestions are included for each technique.

French machine sewing consists of strips of fabric and trims that are sewn together. The fabric strips are embellished with several types of decorative stitching, including machine embroidery, pintucks, and hemstitching. Some of the fabric strips may be gathered to form puffing strips.

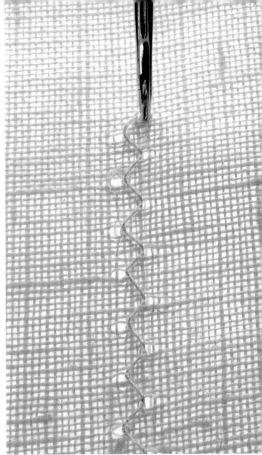

Fagoting creates an open, lacelike effect at a seamline. It can also be used to attach lace edging.

Hemstitching is sewn with a wing needle, making the characteristic "holes" in hemstitched fabric.

Cutwork has open, cutout design areas that are outlined with satin stitching.

Cutwork

Cutwork detailing has open, cutout design areas that are outlined with satin stitching. Cutwork is often used on fine linens or blouses.

Cutwork designs are available, but stencil designs may also be used for cutwork. Both cutwork and stencil designs include bars or bridges, which connect the cutout areas of the cutwork and add stability. If you design your own cutwork, be sure to place bars at frequent intervals. In selecting or planning a cutwork design, keep in mind that it is easier to stitch around large shapes than to follow intricate designs. Select a closely woven fabric that does not ravel easily, such as batiste, chambray, or lightweight linen. All-purpose thread may be used to stitch along the design lines and reinforce the cutout areas; however, for the satin stitching, cotton or rayon machine embroidery thread is recommended. Use a size 70/9 or 80/11 needle.

Stitch the cutwork on the fabric before cutting out the garment section whenever possible. To prevent puckering, place water-soluble stabilizer under the fabric and place the fabric in an embroidery hoop.

How to Sew Cutwork

1) Trace mirror image of design (pages 46 and 47) on water-soluble stabilizer that is cut larger than embroidery hoop. Baste stabilizer to wrong side of fabric. Position fabric in hoop, as on page 103, except, place stabilizer side up.

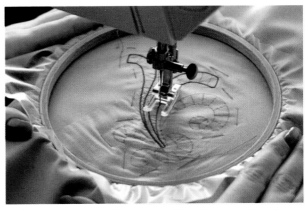

2) Remove presser foot to position hoop under the needle; attach open-toe presser foot. Reinforce outline of design by stitching three rows of straight stitches on design lines, using short stitch length; do not stitch bars.

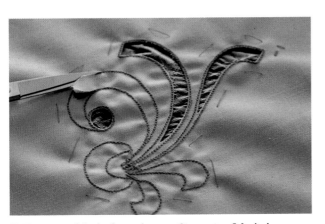

3) Remove fabric from hoop. Cut away fabric in open areas of design 1/16" (1.5 mm) from reinforcement stitches, using embroidery or appliqué scissors; do not cut through the stabilizer. Place fabric, stabilizer side up, in hoop.

4) Stitch three rows of straight stitches on design lines for bars, stitching bars to outer edge of previous rows of outline stitching; second row of stitching can be stitched using reverse setting. Clip threads carried from one design area to another.

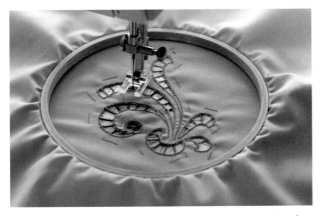

5) Place fabric in hoop right side up. Set machine for zigzag stitching, with stitch width just wide enough to cover straight stitches of bars. Satin stitch over bars.

6) Adjust stitch width so it is wide enough to cover straight stitches and raw edges. Satin stitch cutwork openings so needle stitches just over edge of fabric (pages 74 and 75); work from center of design out, stitching small details first. Remove stabilizer (page 17); press, wrong side up, on padded surface.

How to Satin Stitch Corners and Curves of Cutwork

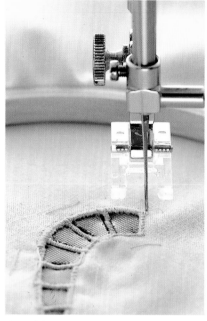

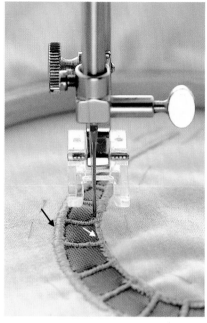

Inside corners. Stitch one stitch past edge of opening, stopping with needle down in stabilizer at inner edge of satin stitching; raise presser foot. Pivot and satin stitch next side of opening, covering previous stitches at corner.

Outside corners. Stitch past corner a distance equal to width of satin stitch, stopping with needle down at outer edge of satin stitching; raise presser foot. Pivot and satin stitch next side of opening, covering previous stitches at corner.

Curves. Raise presser foot and pivot fabric frequently, pivoting with needle down at longest edge of satin stitching (arrows).

How to Satin Stitch Inside Points of Cutwork

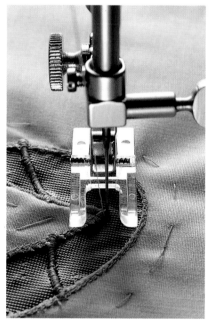

1) Stitch one stitch past the edge of opening, stopping with needle down in stabilizer at inner edge of satin stitching; raise presser foot.

2) Pivot fabric to an angle slightly less than 90°. Stitch two to four stitches, stopping when stitches just cover previous stitches; stop with needle down on inner edge of satin stitching. Raise presser foot.

3) Pivot fabric; continue satin stitching next side of opening.

How to Satin Stitch Outside Points of Cutwork

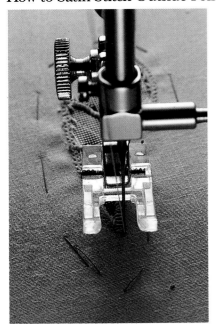

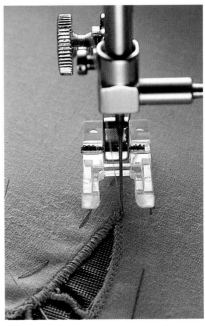

1) Stitch past point a distance equal to width of satin stitch, stopping with needle down at outer edge of satin stitching; raise presser foot.

2) Pivot fabric to an angle slightly less than 90°. Stitch two to four stitches, stopping when stitches just cover previous stitches; stop with needle down on outer edge of satin stitching. Raise presser foot.

3) Pivot fabric; continue satin stitching next side of opening.

How to Satin Stitch Tapered Outside Points

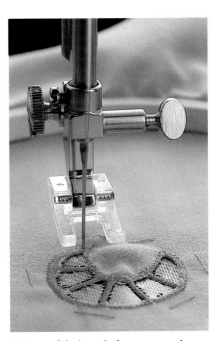

1) Stitch past point a distance equal to width of satin stitch, stopping with needle down at inner edge of satin stitching; raise presser foot.

2) Pivot fabric slightly. Continue stitching, gradually narrowing stitch width to 0 and stopping directly in front of point.

3) Turn fabric; stitch over previous stitches, gradually widening stitch width to original width and stopping at inner edge of satin stitching when stitches meet the finished side of opening. Pivot fabric slightly. Satin stitch next side of opening.

Fagoting

Fagoting is used to create an open, lacelike effect. There are two methods for fagoting, each giving a different appearance. In the first method, curved or straight seamlines are stitched with an open-toe presser foot, using the fagoting stitch or three-step zigzag stitch. This method can be used for attaching lace edging at a hemline or at the outer edge of a collar.

In the second method, a tacking or fringe presser foot and the zigzag stitch are used for straight seamlines only. The width of the fagoting varies from ⅛" to ⅜" (3 mm to 1 cm), depending on the tacking foot; ⅜" (1 cm) fagoting may increase the finished size of the garment slightly. If the bar on the tacking foot is not centered on the foot, use a zigzag stitch with a right-needle position to center the stitches over the bar.

Select the thread and needle according to the weight of the fabric. Cotton machine embroidery thread and a size 70/9 or 80/11 needle will work well for lightweight to mediumweight fabric; rayon thread and a size 80/11 needle may be used if extra sheen is desired. Topstitching thread or buttonhole twist and a size 90/14 needle are recommended for fagoting on mediumweight to heavyweight fabric.

Loosen the needle thread tension, if necessary, so the bobbin thread does not show on the right side of the fabric. Experiment with the stitches on your sewing machine and make a test sample, checking the tension adjustments and stitch length; the shorter the stitch length, the more filled-in the fagoting space.

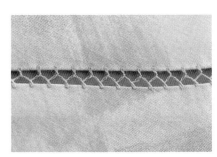

Fagoting stitched using open-toe presser foot.

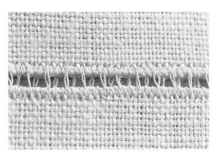

Fagoting stitched using tacking presser foot.

How to Stitch Fagoted Seams Using the Open-toe Foot

1) Trim seam allowances to ¼" (6 mm); finish edges. Press under the seam allowance plus ¹⁄₁₆" (1.5 mm). Baste one folded edge, right side up, to water-soluble stabilizer. Mark a line on stabilizer ⅛" (3 mm) beyond fold. Baste adjoining folded edge to stabilizer at marked line.

2) Center open area under open-toe presser foot. Stitch edges together, using fagoting stitch or 3-step zigzag, barely catching alternate edges as you stitch. Remove stabilizer (page 17); press.

How to Attach Lace Edging with Fagoting Using the Open-toe Foot

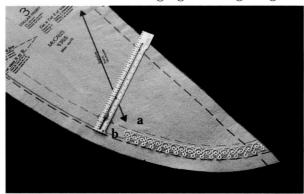

Enclosed seams. 1) Decrease size of pattern by the width of lace edging plus ⅛" (3 mm); mark new seamline **(a),** and cutting line **(b).**

2) Stitch collar; press. Baste outer edge of collar, right side up, to water-soluble stabilizer. Mark line on stabilizer ⅛" (3 mm) beyond edge. Baste straight edge of lace edging to stabilizer at marked line. Stitch fagoting as for seams, step 2, above.

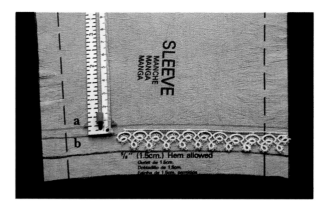

Hemlines. 1) Mark new hemline **(a),** width of lace plus ⅛" (3 mm) from pattern hemline. Mark new cutting line **(b)** ¼" (6 mm) from new hemline.

2) Finish hem edge. Press under ¼" (6 mm). Baste folded edge, right side up, to water-soluble stabilizer. Mark a line on stabilizer ⅛" (3 mm) beyond fold. Baste lace edging to stabilizer at marked line. Stitch fagoting as for seams, step 2, above.

How to Stitch Fagoted Seams Using the Tacking Foot

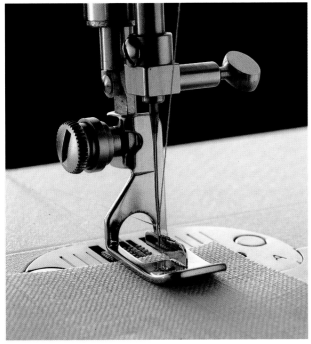

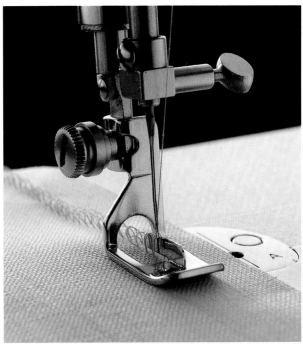

1) Attach tacking foot; place needle thread to back of foot. Set zigzag stitch width so needle barely stitches over bar on foot. If bar is not centered on foot, set machine for zigzag stitch with a right-needle position so stitches are centered over bar. Set stitch length and loosen needle thread tension (page 76).

2) Stitch seam, right sides together, so center of zigzag stitches is ⅝" (1.5 cm) from raw edge.

3) Remove fabric from machine carefully to prevent threads from drawing up. Finish seam allowances. Pull layers apart firmly. Press seam open.

4) Attach open-toe presser foot. Set the machine to balanced tension. Stitch on each side of fagoting, from right side, using satin stitch or other decorative stitch; pull fabric flat as you stitch. If short stitch length is used, the seam allowances may be trimmed close to the stitching.

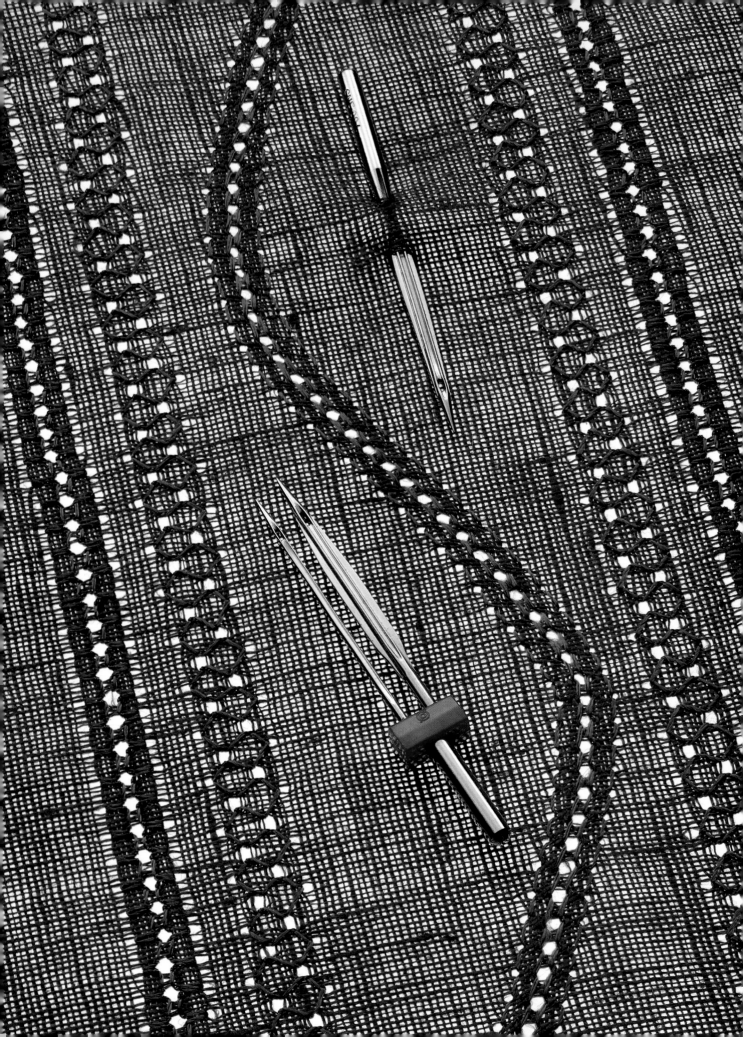

Hemstitching

Traditional hemstitching is done by drawing threads from the fabric and handstitching to produce a lacelike effect, but the same look is easy to duplicate on the conventional sewing machine without drawing threads. Wing needles push the threads aside to produce the characteristic "holes" in the hemstitched fabric. Hemstitching can be used to embellish fabric or to create the look of entredeux when sewing hems and attaching laces.

Two types of wing needles are available: single-wing and double-wing. Single-wing needles are used for sewing either straight, zigzag, or decorative stitches. Sizes range from 90/14 to 120/20; a 120/20 needle makes the largest holes. Double-wing needles are used only to sew straight stitches and feature a wing needle, size 100/16, and a standard needle, size 80/12, on one shank. It is helpful to use an open-toe presser foot when hemstitching.

When using a single-wing needle, test-sew various zigzag, utility, and decorative stitches on your sewing machine, varying the stitch length and stitch width as desired, to determine which stitch patterns you prefer. For more pronounced holes, choose a stitch pattern that allows the wing needle to pierce the same holes more than once. The holes may also be made more pronounced by tightening the tension of the machine slightly, but this may cause some fabrics to pucker.

Hemstitching is most successful on delicate, crisp, natural-fiber fabrics, such as handkerchief linen, organdy, and organza. The fabric must be woven loosely enough so the wing needle can push the threads aside without damaging them, yet must also have enough body so the hole made by the needle does not close immediately after it is pierced. Lightweight fabrics that are more closely woven, such as batiste, may be used, but they may tend to pucker. For best results, use a fine cotton or rayon machine embroidery thread.

To prevent puckering, spray the fabric thoroughly with spray starch and press it before stitching, and, if necessary, place a piece of water-soluble stabilizer under the fabric. Then hold the fabric taut while hemstitching.

If you hemstitch on the crosswise grainline or on the bias, the holes will be more pronounced than if you hemstitch on the lengthwise grainline. It may be necessary to place the pattern pieces on a different grainline when laying out the pattern.

How to Embellish Fabric Using a Single-Wing Needle

1) Apply spray starch to fabric; press. Mark desired stitching lines, using chalk or water-soluble marking pen. Stitch a row of zigzag, utility, or decorative stitches on marked line.

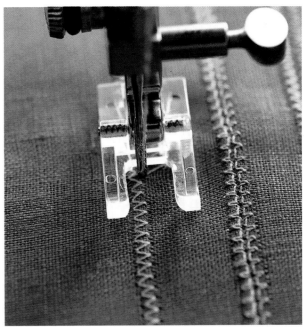

2) Turn fabric at end of stitching and stitch again, if desired, for more pronounced holes. Stitch slowly, making sure needle enters holes exactly on first line of hemstitching.

Hemstitched Laces

When lace trims are attached with hemstitching, the open work formed by the hemstitching enhances the open work of the lace. For a transparent effect, the fabric under the lace is trimmed away close to the hemstitching.

There are two methods for hemstitching laces. The first method is used in areas that will be subjected to stress. Hemstitching is done on a folded edge of fabric and provides extra strength as well as protection against raveling. The alternate method is used for attaching laces that must be eased to follow a curved design, but may also be used for attaching laces in a straight line.

Lightweight lace trims of 100 percent cotton, or of 90 percent cotton and 10 percent nylon, are easy to handle, and shape well. If insertion lace will be eased into curves, select a lace that has gathering threads in the headings, if available. If the lace does not have gathering threads, the edges of the lace can be gathered as on page 94. Apply spray starch to the lace and press it before applying the lace to the garment, to make the lace easier to handle and to prevent puckering.

If the lace is to be hemstitched on the straight of grain, it is recommended that you mark placement lines on the fabric by pulling threads. If the lace will be shaped to follow a curve, placement lines are marked, using a water-soluble marking pen or chalk.

How to Attach Lace Insertion Using Hemstitching

1) Mark placement line, above. Pin lace to fabric at marked line. Stitch lace to fabric, using regular needle and straight stitch; stitch along both headings of lace.

2) Cut down center of fabric under lace, taking care not to cut lace. Press fabric edge on each side away from lace. Change to a single-wing or double-wing needle.

3) Hemstitch, using single-wing needle and zigzag or decorative stitch, with one side of stitch on fabric and other side on lace. Or use double-wing needle and straight stitch, with wing needle on fabric and regular needle on lace.

82

4) Turn fabric at end of stitching and stitch again, if desired, for more pronounced holes; stitch slowly, making sure wing needle enters holes exactly on first line of hemstitching.

5) Repeat steps 3 and 4 for other edge of lace. Trim excess fabric from wrong side, close to stitches.

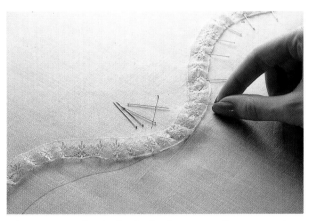

Alternate method. 1) Mark placement line, opposite. If lace requires shaping, pull up gathering threads in lace headings; ease lace to shape of design. Pin lace to fabric at marked line. Press lace flat.

2) Stitch as in steps 1, 3, and 4, on both edges of lace. Trim fabric under lace, from wrong side, close to stitches, taking care not to cut lace.

How to Attach Lace Edging Using Hemstitching

Trim off hem allowance. Place lace edging on right side of fabric, with lower edge of lace at raw edge. Stitch lace heading to fabric, using regular needle and straight stitch; press fabric edge away from lace. Follow steps 3 and 4. Trim excess fabric from wrong side, close to stitches.

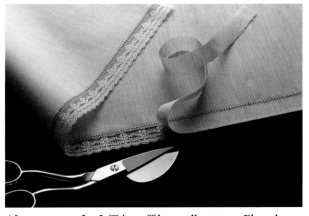

Alternate method. Trim off hem allowance. Place lace edging on right side of fabric, with lower edge of lace at raw edge. Stitch lace heading to fabric, using regular needle and straight stitch. Follow steps 3 and 4. Trim excess fabric from wrong side, close to stitches.

Hemstitched Hems

Hemstitched hems may be either single-fold (top) or double-fold (bottom). For a soft hem with a more sheer appearance, use a single-fold hem. Double-fold hems have more body and appear more opaque.

The technique for single-fold hems can also be used to decoratively secure the raw edge of a facing so it stays neatly in place. Hemstitching also eliminates the need for a seam finish on the facing.

To sew a double-fold hem, double the hem allowance when laying out the pattern. This technique can also be used to hemstitch a cut-on band, such as a band at the center front of a blouse, without the need for interfacing.

How to Sew a Single-fold Hem

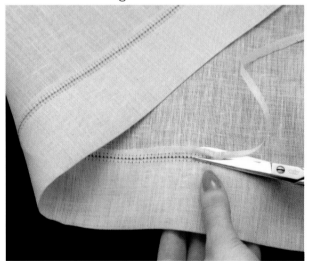

Single-wing needle. Press hem. Using single-wing needle and decorative stitch, stitch from right side ¼" (6 mm) from hem edge. Stitch a second row of stitching as in step 2, opposite, if desired. Trim fabric close to stitches from wrong side.

Double-wing needle. Press hem. Using double-wing needle and straight stitch, stitch from right side ¼" (6 mm) from hem edge. Stitch a second row of stitching as in step 2, opposite, if desired. Trim fabric close to stitches from wrong side.

How to Sew a Double-fold Hem Using a Single-wing Needle

1) Press hem, folding twice. Stitch, using single-wing needle and zigzag or decorative stitch, so one side of stitch pierces hem allowance and other side of stitch pierces single layer of fabric.

2) Turn fabric at end of stitching and stitch again, if desired, for more pronounced holes. Stitch slowly, making sure wing needle enters holes exactly on first line of hemstitching.

How to Sew a Double-fold Hem Using a Double-wing Needle

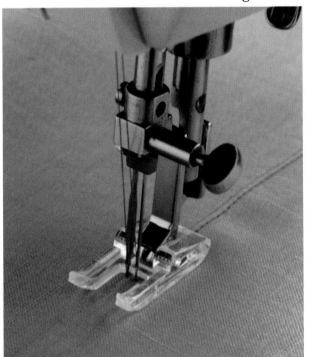

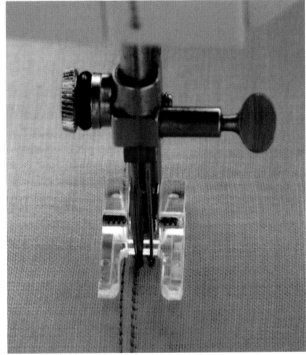

1) Press hem, folding twice. Stitch from right side, using double-wing needle and straight stitch so standard needle pierces hem allowance and wing needle pierces single layer of fabric.

2) Turn fabric at end of stitching and stitch again, if desired, for more pronounced holes. Stitch slowly, making sure needle enters holes exactly on first line of hemstitching.

Pintucks

Pintucks are one of the most versatile decorative effects. They can be a demure accent on a feminine blouse or a tailored treatment on a crisp shirt. They can also add interest to pillows and table linens.

Traditionally stitched pintucks (top), are stitched near a folded edge and are suitable for lightweight to mediumweight even-weave fabrics. Two variations of the traditional pintuck are decoratively stitched pintucks (middle) and twisted pintucks (bottom).

Pintucks are less likely to pucker if they are stitched on the crosswise grain of the fabric. It is better to sew all the pintucks before cutting out the garment piece unless you are using a pattern that includes pintucks.

Pintucks can be as narrow as ¹⁄₁₆" (1.5 mm) on lightweight fabrics. On mediumweight fabrics, make the pintucks ¹⁄₈" (3 mm), so they will lie flat when pressed to one side. Depending on the width of the presser foot, you may be able to guide the foldline of the fabric along the inner edge of the presser foot for ¹⁄₈" (3 mm) pintucks. On some machines, you can move the needle to a right-needle position to guide a ¹⁄₁₆" (1.5 mm) pintuck.

How to Sew Traditionally Stitched Pintucks

1) Measure size and spacing of all pintucks on fabric; allow ⅛" (3 mm) to ¼" (6 mm) to be taken up by each tuck. Pull threads to mark foldlines of tucks, or mark foldlines with chalk.

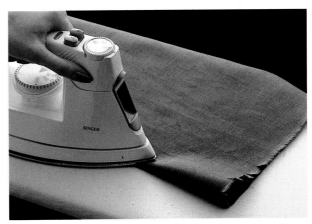

2) Fold and press fabric, wrong sides together, on foldline for each pintuck.

3) Stitch ⅟₁₆" to ⅛" (1.5 to 3 mm) from foldline of first pintuck, using straight stitches. Press pintuck with needle thread up.

4) Stitch remaining pintucks in same direction as first pintuck to prevent distortion; press.

How to Sew Decoratively Stitched Pintucks

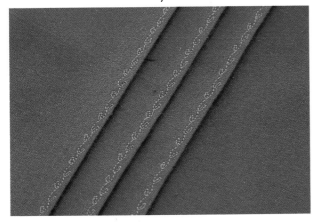

Stitch ⅛" (3 mm) traditionally stitched pintucks, above, using decorative stitch set at narrow stitch width, instead of straight stitch.

How to Sew Twisted Pintucks

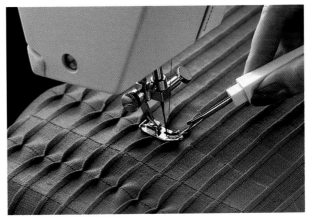

Stitch and press ⅛" (3 mm) traditionally stitched pintucks, above. Mark evenly spaced rows across pintucks; topstitch, reversing the direction of tucks with each row. Use seam ripper or screwdriver to change direction of pintucks as you stitch.

French Machine Sewing

French machine sewing consists of stitching strips of fabric and trims together. These strips may be placed either horizontally or vertically on the garment piece, and they may vary in width, as desired.

The fabric strips may be embellished with machine embroidery, pintucks, or hemstitching, or they may be gathered to make puffing strips. The strips are pieced together to create heirloom fabric before the pattern is laid out. Use French machine sewing to embellish areas such as a yoke, collar, blouse front, or skirt hem. The best styles to choose are those with few darts and seams.

All-cotton Swiss batiste, available in three weights, is the traditional fabric choice for French machine sewing; its wrinkles are merely part of its appeal. Other batistes and broadcloths in cotton or cotton blends are also suitable. Imperial® batiste, for example, is an economical polyester/cotton blend that is wrinkle-resistant.

Lace trims of 100 percent cotton, or of 90 percent cotton and 10 percent nylon, feel soft and are easy to handle. You may use insertion lace or lace edging. Lace beading, with double-faced satin ribbon woven through the beading, adds special detailing.

Entredeux is a trim that resembles hemstitching, with seam allowances on both sides. It is used between fabric strips and laces to reinforce seams decoratively.

For sewing lightweight fabrics and trims, use a 50-weight or 60-weight cotton machine embroidery thread, because it will not add bulk to the seams. Or if extra sheen is desired, fine rayon thread may be used. White thread is appropriate for sewing white, ecru, or pastel fabrics; the fine white thread blends into the fabric.

A sharp, new needle in size 70/9 is essential for machine heirloom sewing. Change the needle after every few hours of sewing, even if the point of the needle feels smooth.

You may want to practice the heirloom techniques on pages 90 to 94 before making your project.

Pillow of Swiss cotton features pintucks, puffing strips, decorative stitching, and delicate Swiss laces. Lace beading is accented with narrow satin ribbons.

How to Design a French Machine Sewing Project

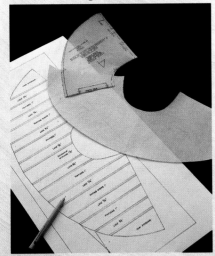

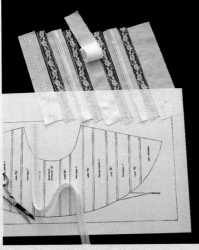

1) Make a full-size pattern piece from tissue; trace onto firm paper. Plan design, using entredeux, lace trims, and fabric strips. Entredeux should be between all strips of fabric and lace; fabric strips should be at ends, if edges are curved.

2) Measure pattern at its widest and longest points. Embellish and cut strips (page 90); finished length of the strips should be 1" (2.5 cm) longer than width or length of the pattern, depending on the direction of the strips.

3) Stitch entredeux, lace trims, and fabric strips together (pages 92 to 94) to form rectangle or square. Block fabric and cut out garment piece (page 95).

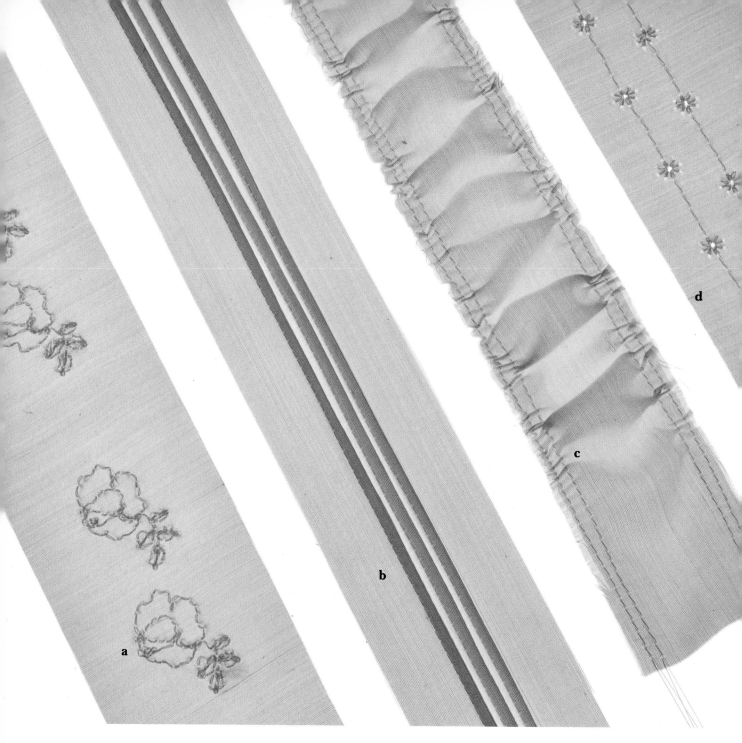

Making the Heirloom Strips

Make heirloom strips by embellishing strips of fabric with decorative machine stitching **(a),** pintucks **(b),** gathering or puffing **(c),** or hemstitching **(d).**

The fabric strips are cut or torn on the straight of grain; seams are less likely to pucker when strips are cut or torn on the crosswise grain. Each strip is cut ½" (1.3 cm) wider than the desired finished width to allow for seam allowances; allow additional width for pintucks. Cut puffing strips 1½ times longer than the

pattern piece to allow for gathering. Cut other strips 1" (2.5 cm) longer than the pattern piece.

Apply spray starch to all fabric strips, except puffing strips, to make the fabric easier to handle. To prevent scorching, spray the starch on the wrong side of the fabric and press from the right side. For puffing strips, press, but do not starch, the fabric strips before gathering them. To prevent flattening the gathers, puffing strips should not be pressed with an iron after they are sewn; they may be finger-pressed.

How to Prepare Straight-grain Fabric Strips

Swiss cotton. Clip into selvage. To straighten end of fabric, pull a thread across to other selvage; cut on pulled thread line. Clip again and pull a thread at desired width of each fabric strip, opposite; cut on pulled thread line.

Cotton/polyester batiste. Clip selvage and tear fabric to straighten end. Clip again and tear at desired width of each fabric strip, opposite; press flat. Trim torn edges, if desired, using rotary cutter and ruler.

How to Sew Puffing Strips

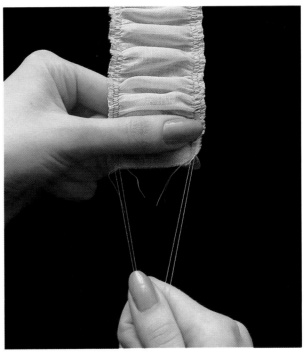

1) Cut fabric strips, above. Set stitch length to 12 stitches per inch (2.5 cm); loosen needle thread tension. Stitch two rows of gathering threads on each long side of strip, with rows ⅛" (3 mm) and a scant ¼" (6 mm) from edge.

2) Pull up gathering threads on each side of puffing strip, gathering strip evenly to desired length. Knot gathering threads at each end.

Joining the Heirloom Strips

Fabric strips, laces, and trims for French machine sewing are stitched together with narrow seams that are neat and durable. A technique called rolling and whipping is often used; the seam allowances actually roll or curl and are secured with zigzag stitches.

When flat lace edging or insertion lace is rolled and whipped to a fabric strip, the extended fabric rolls over the lace edge. When flat lace is applied at a hem edge, the rolled-and-whipped seam may be pressed toward the fabric and edgestitched through all layers.

Entredeux is frequently used between fabrics and laces to reinforce the seams. For a decorative effect, lace beading and entredeux can be embellished by weaving narrow ribbon or embroidery floss through the holes of the trim.

Gather flat lace, if desired, before stitching it to trimmed entredeux. If both edges of the entredeux are trimmed off, the gathered lace and entredeux can be used to highlight a yoke seam or neck edge.

How to Set the Machine Stitch Length

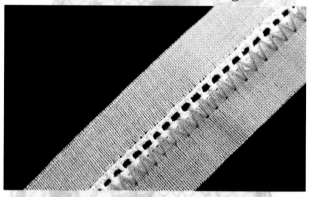

Cut a test strip of entredeux about 4" (10 cm) long. Set stitch width of zigzag stitch 3 mm wide; set stitch length for 16 to 18 stitches per inch (2.5 cm). Then adjust stitch length until needle stitches into each hole of the entredeux. This stitch length is used for the entire project.

How to Sew a Fabric Strip to Flat Lace Using Rolling and Whipping

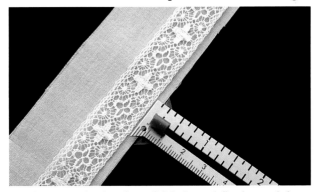

1) Place starched strips of fabric and flat lace, right sides together, with lace on top and fabric extending ⅛" (3 mm) to right of lace.

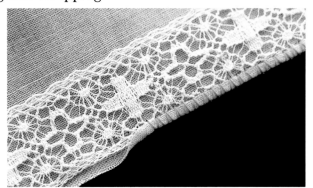

2) Set stitch width of zigzag stitch so left swing of needle stitches to the left of lace heading and right swing extends over raw edge of fabric strip. As needle moves to the left, edge of fabric rolls over lace; if fabric does not roll, adjust needle thread tension. Press seam toward fabric.

How to Sew a Fabric Strip to Entredeux Using Rolling and Whipping

1) Trim seam allowance of entredeux to ¼" (6 mm). Place starched strips of fabric and entredeux, right sides together, with raw edges even. Stitch next to entredeux holes; trim seam allowances to ⅛" (3 mm).

2) Set stitch width of zigzag stitch so left swing of needle stitches in ditch of entredeux and right swing extends over raw edges. As needle moves to the left, edges of strips roll; if fabric does not roll, adjust the needle thread tension. Press seam toward fabric.

How to Sew a Puffing Strip to Entredeux Using Rolling and Whipping

1) Trim seam allowance of entredeux to ¼" (6 mm). Place puffing strip and starched entredeux, right sides together, with raw edges even. Stitch next to entredeux holes; trim seam allowances to ⅛" (3 mm).

2) Set stitch width of zigzag stitch so left swing of needle stitches in ditch of entredeux and right swing extends over raw edges. As needle moves to the left, edges of strips roll slightly; if fabric does not roll, adjust needle thread tension. Press seam toward fabric, using tip of iron; do not press puffing strip flat.

How to Sew Flat Lace Trims Together

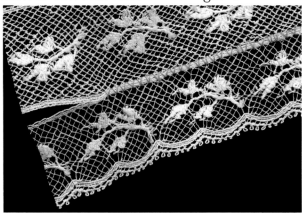

Butt edges of laces, right sides up. Set stitch length (page 92); zigzag, using a narrow stitch width.

How to Sew a Flat Lace Trim to Entredeux

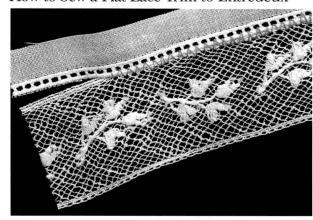

Trim away one seam allowance of entredeux. Butt trimmed edge of entredeux to edge of lace. Set stitch length (page 92); zigzag, using a narrow stitch width. Stitch into the center of entredeux holes.

How to Gather a Flat Lace Trim and Sew to Entredeux

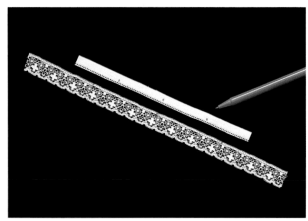

1) Cut entredeux 1" (2.5 cm) longer than needed; trim away one seam allowance. Cut flat lace 1½ times longer than entredeux. Divide lace and entredeux into fourths; mark.

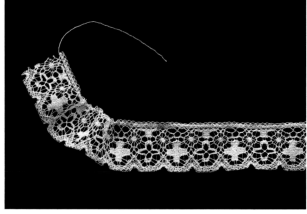

2a) Lace with gathering thread in heading. Pull the gathering thread in heading from both ends to gather lace; some laces have several gathering threads, in case of breakage. Match marks on lace and entredeux.

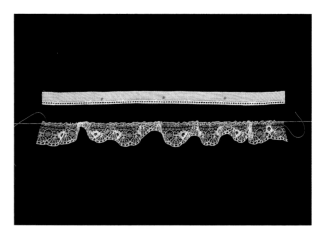

2b) Lace without gathering thread in heading. Stitch next to lace edge, using 10 to 12 stitches per inch (2.5 cm); pull bobbin thread to gather. Match marks on lace and entredeux.

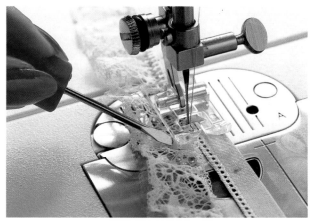

3) Butt trimmed edge of entredeux to lace. Set stitch length (page 92); zigzag, using a narrow stitch width. Guide gathers under presser foot, using a small screwdriver. Remove gathering thread.

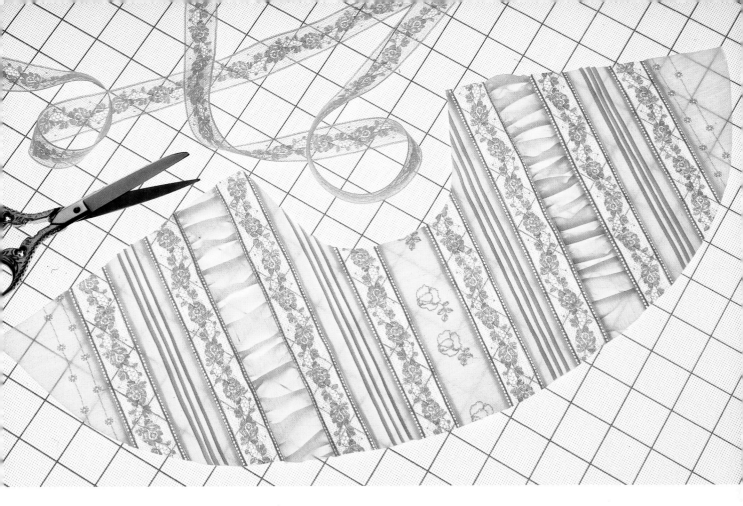

Cutting the Heirloom Fabric

Block the completed heirloom fabric to set the shape before cutting the garment pieces. The fabric is pinned to a padded surface, such as an ironing board, so the seams are straight. Then the fabric is steamed, taking care not to flatten any machine embroidery or puffing strips. After the blocked fabric has cooled, place the full-size pattern pieces on the fabric (page 89), matching the planned design as closely as possible.

How to Block and Cut the Heirloom Pieces

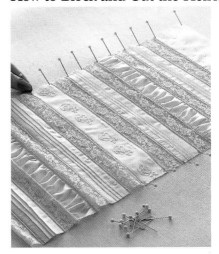

1) Pin heirloom fabric to padded surface so seams are straight.

2) Steam fabric to set shape, taking care not to flatten puffing strips or machine embroidery. Allow fabric to cool before removing pins.

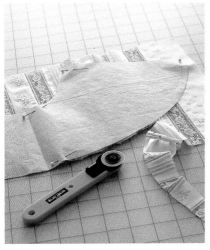

3) Position pattern piece on fabric, centering it on middle strip; seams of strips may not match planned design exactly. Cut garment piece.

Finishing the Heirloom Garment

French seams and French bindings are used for seam finishes in delicate heirloom garments. French seams are used only for straight seams. French bindings are used for curved seams, such as armhole seams of set-in sleeves, opposite. They are also used for seams with gathers, such as gathered waistlines.

Eliminate facings whenever possible, and bind the edges of the neckline and sleeveless armholes with French binding. Or use lace and entredeux at the neckline as a pretty finish; attach the lace to the entredeux, as on page 94, and then sew the entredeux to the garment edge, as on page 93.

Rolling and whipping may be used for a narrow hem finish on a ruffle or at the lower edge of a garment.

How to Sew Narrow French Seams

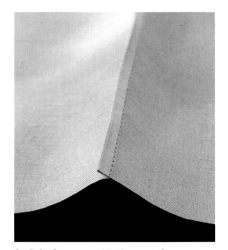

1) Place garment pieces with *wrong* sides together. Stitch seam, within the seam allowance, ³⁄₁₆" (4.5 mm) from the seamline, using 16 to 18 stitches per inch (2.5 cm).

2) Trim seam allowances to scant ⅛" (3 mm); press seam allowances to one side. Fold on stitching line, right sides together; press.

3) Stitch seam ⅛" (3 mm) from fold, encasing raw edges. Press seam allowance to one side.

How to Finish Seams and Edges with French Binding

Seams. 1) Cut 1¾" (4.5 cm) bias strip of lightweight fabric 1" (2.5 cm) longer than edge. Press the strip in half lengthwise, wrong sides together. Trim seam allowances on garment to scant ¼" (6 mm).

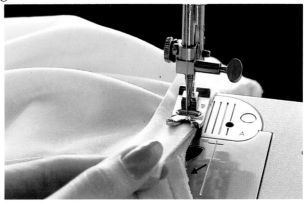

2) Pin binding to garment, raw edges even. Stitch, using ¼" (6 mm) seam; stretch binding slightly on inside curves. For continuous edge, tuck ½" (1.3 cm) to inside of binding at beginning of strip (arrow). For edge at garment opening, wrap ½" (1.3 cm) of binding around ends.

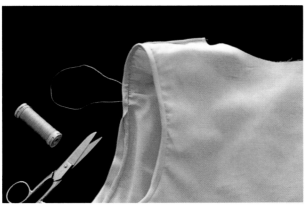

3) Press binding toward seam allowances. Fold the binding in half over raw edges; pin. Slipstitch folded edge of binding to previous stitching line. Press.

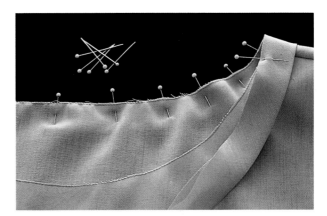

Edges. Staystitch just beyond the seamline to prevent stretching; trim at seamline. Cut and press bias strip, as in step 1. Pin binding to right side of garment, raw edges even; attach as in steps 2 and 3.

How to Sew a Narrow Hem Using Rolling and Whipping

1) Staystitch bias edges ¼" (6 mm) from edge; then trim fabric close to stitching. It is not necessary to staystitch edges that are on the straight of grain.

2) Set stitch width to 12 to 16 stitches per inch (2.5 cm); set stitch width so left swing of needle stitches ⅛" (3 mm) from raw edge and right swing of needle extends over raw edge. As needle moves to the left, edge of fabric will roll.

Free-motion Sewing

Free-motion Machine Embroidery

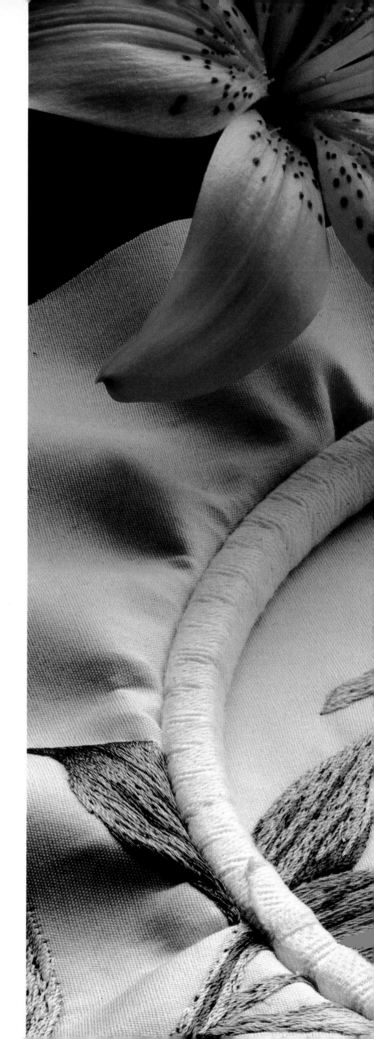

Free-motion machine embroidery offers opportunities for creativity that are not possible with the decorative stitches on your sewing machine. Use free-motion embroidery for thread painting on garments and home decorating projects, for monogramming on towels and garments, and for making Battenberg lace.

In free-motion sewing, the presser foot is removed and the feed dogs are covered with a cover plate, or lowered. The fabric is moved freely under the sewing machine needle to create a design. At first, you may feel awkward, because you feed the fabric through the machine manually instead of using the feed dog system. With practice, you will be able to slide the fabric smoothly as you stitch. You control the stitch length. Create stitches that are close together by moving the fabric slowly as you stitch.

The fabric is held taut in a 5" to 7" (12.5 to 18 cm) embroidery hoop. A wooden hoop with a fixing screw works best because it can be tightened firmly. Select a hoop that is ¼" (6 mm) thick so it will slide easily under the sewing machine needle. The hoop should also be smooth, with beveled edges, so it does not snag the fabric or scratch the bed of the sewing machine.

For best results, use machine embroidery thread (page 14). It is available in cotton, rayon, and metallic, in weights ranging from 30-weight to 60-weight. Larger design areas are filled in more quickly when heavier, 30-weight, thread is used. Finer threads fill in areas more smoothly, without thread buildup, and reduce fabric puckering. Cotton basting thread or fine monofilament nylon thread may be used in the bobbin instead of machine embroidery thread. It is not necessary for the bobbin thread to match the color of the needle thread.

You may find it necessary to use tear-away stabilizer under the fabric to prevent puckering, especially if the embroidery design area is large. Stabilizers also help prevent thread breakage and skipped stitches. It is not necessary to place the stabilizer in the hoop with the fabric; it can be placed under the hoop as you stitch.

Use a sharp, new needle for machine embroidery. Even a slightly damaged or dull needle can cause broken threads or skipped stitches. For sewing with cotton machine embroidery thread, use a fine needle in size 70/9 or 80/11. Use a size 80/11 or 90/14 with rayon machine embroidery thread.

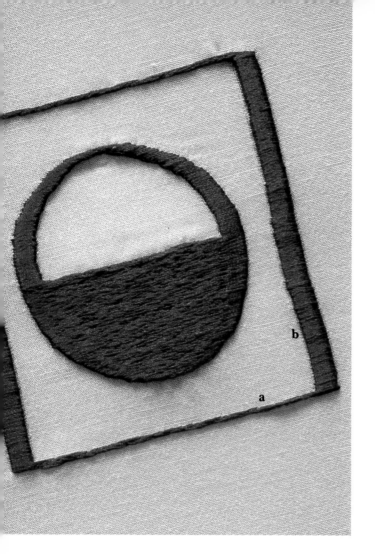

Getting Ready to Sew

To prevent the fabric from loosening or slipping while stitching, wrap the inner ring of the embroidery hoop with cotton twill tape, or glue velvet ribbon to the outside edge of the inner ring. Then position the fabric firmly in the hoop.

To become familiar with the techniques of free-motion embroidery, it is helpful to practice sewing the side stitch **(a)** and satin stitch **(b).** The side stitch is formed as you move the fabric sideways; the width of the side stitches is determined by the stitch width setting and the density of the embroidery. The satin stitch is sewn as you move the fabric slowly toward you or away from you; the width of the satin stitches is determined by the stitch width setting.

The circle and square design is helpful for learning the basic techniques. Use machine embroidery thread (page 14) when you are practicing and adjust the tension of the machine, if necessary, so the bobbin thread does not show on the right side of the fabric (page 18).

It is easier to sew in free motion if you are relaxed. Rest your hands comfortably on the sides of the embroidery hoop; do not grip the hoop. Run the machine at a moderate to fast speed, but move the hoop slowly as you stitch, so the stitches will be close together and filled in.

How to Prepare the Embroidery Hoop

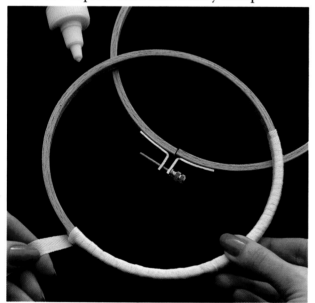

Twill tape method. Secure one end of narrow, cotton twill tape to inner ring of hoop with fabric glue. Wrap ring in diagonal direction, overlapping tape by half its width; pull firmly while wrapping. Secure other end of tape with glue. Allow glue to dry before using the hoop.

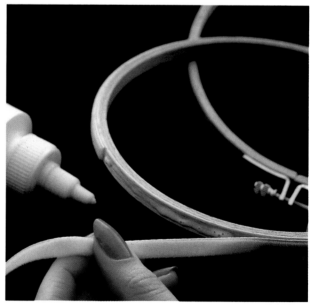

Velvet ribbon method. Secure ¼" (6 mm) velvet ribbon with fabric glue to outside edge of inner ring. Allow glue to dry before using hoop.

How to Prepare the Practice Fabric

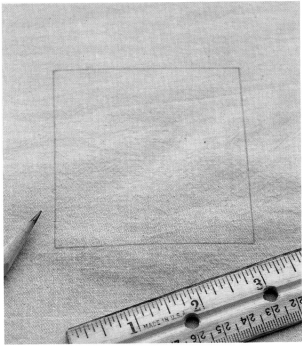

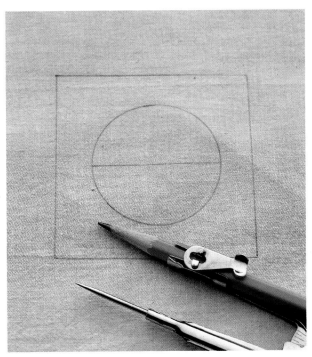

1) Cut 12" (30.5 cm) square of muslin or organdy. In center of fabric, draw a 3" (7.5 cm) square, using a lead pencil or water-soluble or fine-tip permanent marking pen.

2) Draw 2" (5 cm) diameter circle inside the square; draw horizon line through center of circle; this line must be kept horizontal at all times as you sew.

How to Position the Fabric in the Embroidery Hoop

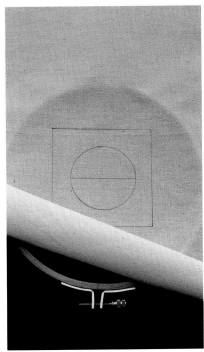

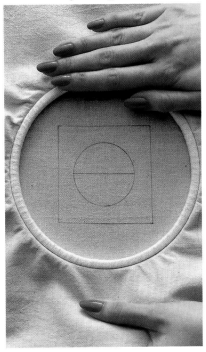

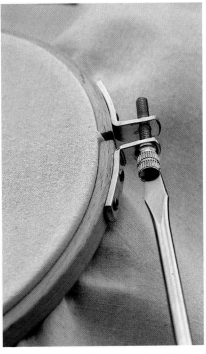

1) Loosen the fixing screw of hoop slightly with screwdriver to separate rings. Place outer ring on table, with screw facing toward you. Place the fabric over the hoop, right side up, centering design.

2) Push inner ring into outer ring with heels of your palms, making sure fabric is taut. Partially tighten screw and gently pull fabric edges evenly until fabric is very taut; do not distort grainline.

3) Push inner ring to underside about ⅛" (3 mm); this helps to tighten fabric. Tighten screw with screwdriver to prevent fabric from slipping or loosening as you stitch.

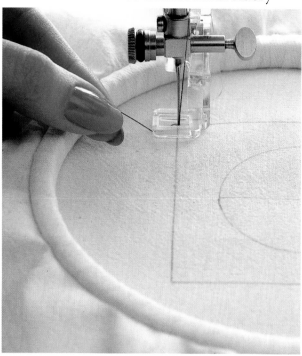

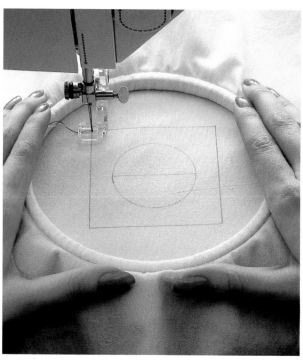

1) Adjust tension (page 18). Cover feed dogs with cover plate or lower them. Attach darning foot. Set stitch width to 0. Draw up bobbin thread at upper left corner of square. Holding threads, stitch in place a few times to secure stitches.

2) Set stitch width to wide setting. Rest hands on sides of hoop; do not grip hoop. Sit comfortably, directly in front of needle.

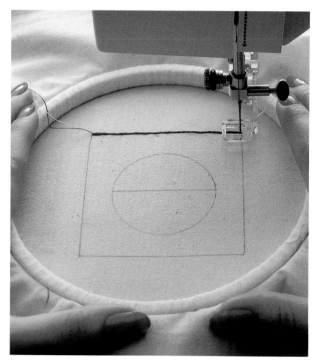

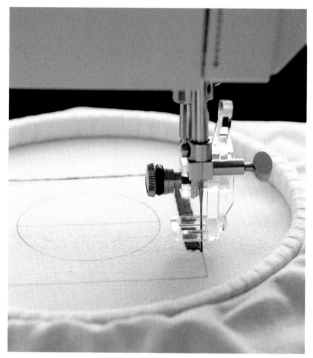

3) Stitch at moderately fast speed, moving hoop sideways slowly to sew side stitch. Clip thread tails from starting point.

4) Stitch at moderately fast speed, moving hoop away from you to sew satin stitch. Practice stitching so fabric does not show between the stitches; stitch back over the previous stitches to fill in, as necessary. (Darning foot was raised to show detail.)

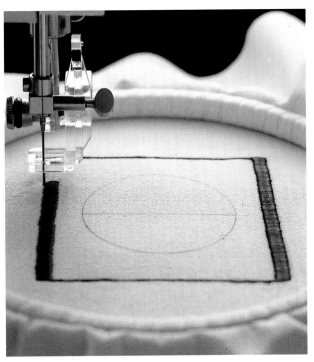

5) Continue around square, moving hoop sideways to sew side stitch. Then move hoop toward you to sew satin stitch on last line of square. Set stitch width to 0 and secure stitches.

6) Lift darning foot; pull threads to edge of circle near horizon line. Set stitch width to 0 and secure stitches; reset stitch width to wide setting. Move hoop smoothly sideways, forward, or backward as you stitch around circle. Do not turn hoop; keep horizon line horizontal. Set stitch width to 0 and secure stitches.

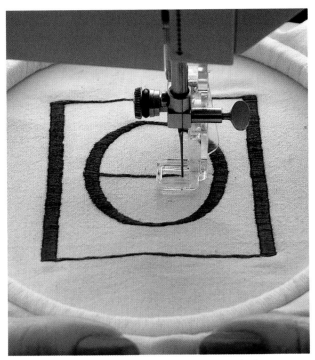

7) Clip needle thread carried from outer design area. Set stitch width to wide setting. Stitch across horizon line, using side stitch.

8) Continue stitching rows from side to side across circle, with each row next to the previous row, until one half of circle is filled in; allow stitches to run into outline of circle to prevent a line around circle. Stitch other half of circle.

Thread Sketching

Thread sketching is done by stitching with the needle as if you were using a pencil to draw lines. Use free-motion techniques and the straight stitch.

Thread painting looks similar to hand embroidery fill-in stitches. Free-motion machine embroidery techniques are used to fill in an entire design area with thread. For the fill-in stitches, use the zigzag stitch in a stitch width that is appropriate for each design area. Change the stitch width, as necessary, from one area to another.

Tips for Thread Sketching and Thread Painting

Use needle to thread-sketch marked design lines on fabric or to sketch free-form shapes.

Draw directional or horizon lines as a guide for filling in areas of the design with thread painting.

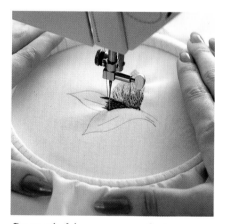

Start stitching on areas that are farthest away from you or those that appear to be under other areas.

Thread Painting

Both techniques can be used to embellish solid-color fabric or to emphasize the design of a printed fabric, adding texture and dimension to the fabric. The basic free-motion techniques on pages 100 to 105 are used for both thread painting and thread sketching. Set the stitch width to 0 and stitch in place a few times to secure the stitches when moving from one area to another, or when changing thread colors.

How to Shade Areas in Thread Painting

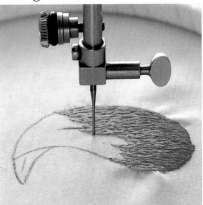

1) Stitch in place at edge of design area, such as base of petal or leaf. Outline and fill in portion of design for first thread color, working from base out; leave a jagged edge for blending in next color. Stitch in place at end to secure stitches.

2) Change thread color; stitch in place at jagged edge of design area. Using fill-in stitches, stitch second color, blending into jagged, open areas of first color. Continue blending new colors along edges of previous colors to complete design.

3) Use a dark, contrasting thread color to add accent stitching, if desired. Using narrow zigzag stitch or straight stitch, sew along edge of design and on design lines, such as veins in leaf.

Monograms

Although the automatic monogram stitch patterns on computerized sewing machines are convenient and easy to stitch, you may want to create different sizes or styles of monograms, using free-motion machine embroidery.

Monograms can either be drawn directly onto the fabric or onto a piece of water-soluble stabilizer. If you are monogramming a bath towel or sweater, it is easier to draw the monogram on water-soluble stabilizer than it is to draw it on the textured fabric; the stabilizer is then placed over the fabric to use as a guide for stitching. Draw a horizon line under each letter and keep it horizontal as you stitch so the stitching will automatically taper in the right places.

Use a narrow, wooden hoop or a spring hoop (page 16) for monogramming. Wooden hoops with fixing screws hold the fabric more tightly, but spring hoops are available in the small sizes needed for areas such as pockets, cuffs, and collars. It is helpful to place tear-away stabilizer under the hoop to prevent the fabric from puckering.

You can use either 30-weight or 40-weight machine embroidery thread for monogramming; the 30-weight thread is a little heavier and fills in faster than 40-weight thread.

Practice stitching the upper case "M" and lower case "e", because these two letters include all the techniques required for the other letters in the alphabet. When you monogram, think of the sewing machine needle as a pencil. Start to stitch each letter at the same place you would start writing it with a pencil.

The size of the letter determines the stitch width; the larger the letter, the wider the stitch width. The widest stitch width setting on the sewing machine works well for 2" (5 cm) letters, but a medium stitch width should be used for smaller letters.

How to Stitch an Upper Case "M" Monogram

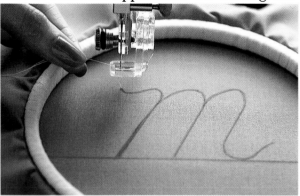

1) Draw an upper case "M" about 2" (5 cm) high on fabric; draw horizon line under letter. Place fabric in embroidery hoop (page 103). Set stitch width to 0. Draw up bobbin thread at top of "M"; stitch in place a few times to secure stitches. Set stitch width to the widest setting.

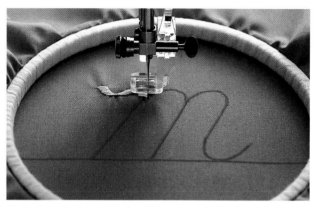

2) Satin stitch up to the first stem of the letter, using short zigzag stitches; keep horizon line horizontal as you sew.

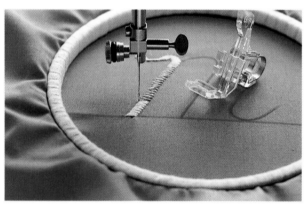

3) Stitch down the first stem of the letter, using longer zigzag stitches, to prevent a buildup of stitches on the stem. Satin stitch back over the stem, using short, closely spaced zigzag stitches. (Darning foot was removed to show detail.)

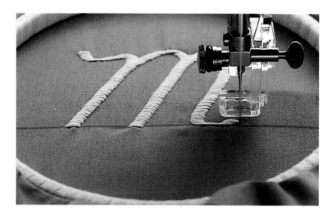

4) Continue satin stitching to second stem of letter; repeat step 3 for second stem. Satin stitch remainder of letter. Set stitch width to 0 and secure stitches.

How to Stitch a Lower Case "e" Monogram

1) Draw lower case "e" about 1" (2.5 cm) high on fabric; draw horizon line under letter. Place fabric in embroidery hoop. Set stitch width to 0. Draw up bobbin thread at left side of "e"; secure stitches. Set stitch width to a medium setting.

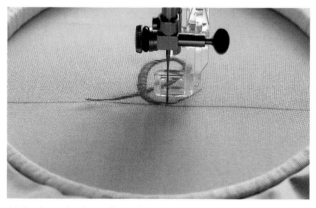

2) Satin stitch, using short, closely spaced zigzag stitches; stitch on the outside of loop so center of loop does not become too small. Keep the horizon line horizontal as you sew. Set the stitch width to 0 and secure stitches.

Tips for Monogramming

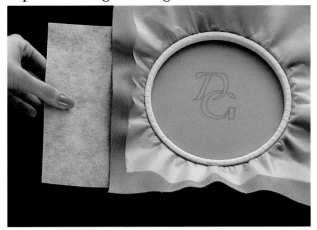

Trace letters on water-soluble stabilizer. Place the stabilizer on right side of fabric; position in hoop. Place tear-away stabilizer under hoop during stitching. Remove both stabilizers after stitching (page 17).

Change direction of the horizon line, such as placing it on the diagonal, so tapering of letter changes position for a different look.

Change direction of the horizon line within a letter for added emphasis.

Change stitch width as you stitch the letters for an interesting effect. Change the width when sewing side stitch or at top of letter so width change is less noticeable and flows with the letter.

Stitch larger letters first with narrower stitches; then repeat stitching with wider stitches if raised or padded effect is desired.

Use wide stitch width for large letters and a narrower stitch width for small letters.

Floral Monograms

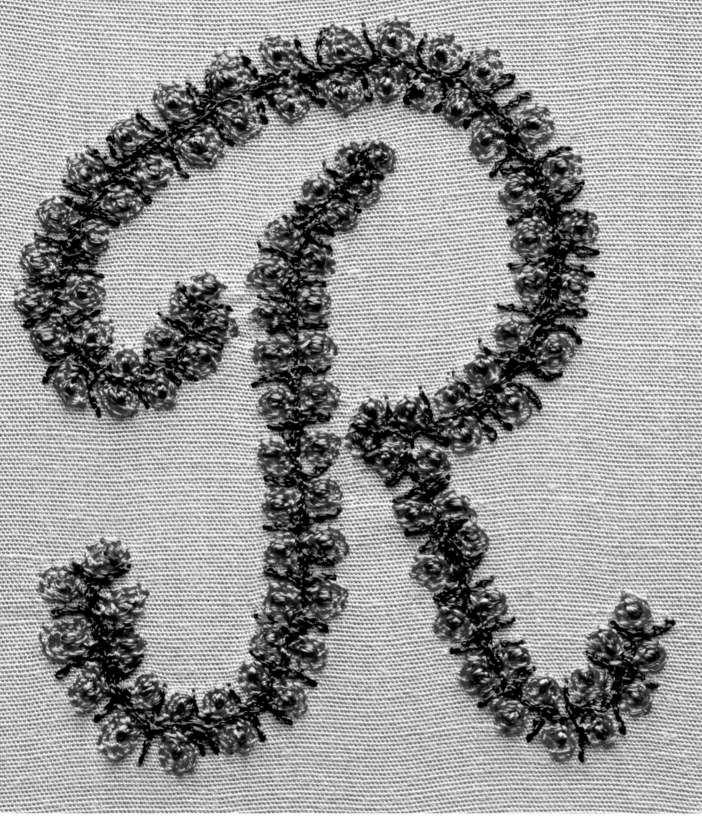

The floral monogram is made up of small flowers and leaves, and is sewn using free-motion embroidery techniques (pages 100 to 105).

Letter styles that have smooth, curved lines are more appropriate for floral monograms than block styles. Select dark and light colors of thread to stitch the flowers and a green thread for the leaves.

How to Make Free-motion Floral Monograms

1) Draw 2" or 2½" (5 or 6.5 cm) letter on fabric with water-soluble marking pen. Draw small dots on each side of letter about ¼" (6 mm) apart; dots may be placed closer together on curves. Place fabric in the embroidery hoop.

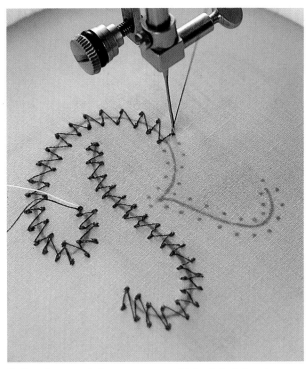

2) Set zigzag stitch to narrow width. Stitch in place on dot five or six times, using a dark-colored thread. Move across marked line to next dot; stitch in place. Continue until all dots are stitched, to make centers of flowers. Clip thread tails, but do not clip threads between dots.

3) Set machine for straight stitch; change to lighter-colored thread. Stitch around center of one flower; continue until all flowers are stitched. Clip thread tails, but do not clip threads between flowers.

4) Change to green thread. Using the straight stitch setting on machine, stitch leaves in curved motion, stitching in and out between the flowers.

Battenberg Lace

Battenberg lace, which has been made by hand since the seventeenth century, can now be made using machine embroidery techniques on the sewing machine. The lace is made using a decorative tape, called Battenberg tape, that is arranged and pinned to water-soluble stabilizer. The open areas in the design are embellished with fill-in stitches, using a balanced tension on the machine and free-motion stitching techniques (pages 100 to 105).

The two types of Battenberg tape, flat-edge and picot-edge, are available in various widths and colors. The straight edges of Battenberg tape have a heavy cord, or gimp, that is pulled to shape the tape as it curves. Battenberg tape does not have a right or a wrong side, so it can be folded back on itself to shape points or corners.

Patterns for Battenberg designs are available from pattern companies and from some fabric stores and craft stores. Also, patterns are included in some magazines that specialize in lacemaking.

If you are using a pattern designed for Battenberg lace, the yardage requirements for the tape will be listed in the pattern. Or you can determine the yardage by measuring the design, as shown below. Keep the Battenberg tape in workable lengths of one to two yards (0.95 to 1.85 m); tape can be pieced at any point in the design where the tape overlaps.

The stitching is done with machine embroidery thread that matches the Battenberg tape. Use the same thread in both the needle and the bobbin. A 50-weight or 60-weight cotton thread should be used to secure the tape to the stabilizer and a 30-weight cotton or rayon thread for the fill-in stitches. A size 70/9 or 80/11 needle is recommended for use with machine embroidery thread; do not use a needle smaller than a size 80/11 with rayon thread.

Use a 6" to 10" (15 to 25.5 cm) wooden embroidery hoop with a fixing screw, or a spring hoop; the spring hoop may not stretch or distort the tape as much as the wooden hoop. The hoop may be wrapped with twill tape (page 102) to help hold the stabilizer taut. For larger pieces of lace, you may need to move the hoop to stitch the lace in sections.

Types of Battenberg Tape

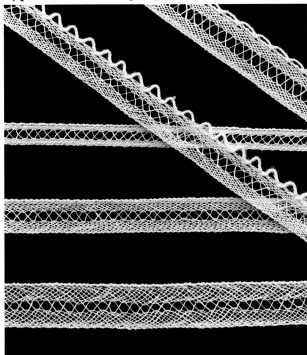

Battenberg tape is available in two types: straight-edge tape with two straight edges, and picot-edge tape with one picot and one straight edge.

How to Calculate Yardage for Battenberg Tape

Measure around design, standing tape measure on its edge. Add 3" (7.5 cm) to this measurement for finishing the ends.

How to Make Battenberg Lace

1) Position water-soluble stabilizer in embroidery hoop (page 103). Pin pattern for lace to foam board or Styrofoam®; place hoop over pattern. Trace design on stabilizer, using either a water-soluble or a permanent marking pen. Remove pattern.

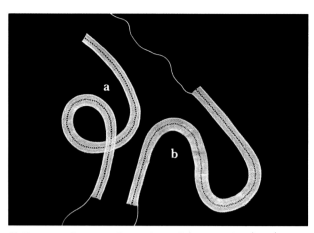

2) Locate gimp cord at edge of tape. Pull out 15" to 20" (38 to 51 cm) of gimp; gather tape, leaving first several inches flat. For designs with inside curves, pull gimp on one edge only **(a).** For designs with inside and outside curves, pull gimp on both edges, pulling from opposite ends of tape **(b).**

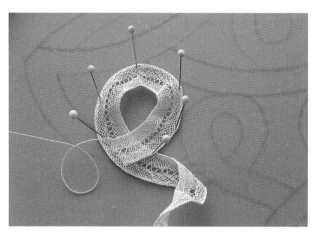

3) Pin outer edge of tape through stabilizer to foam board in shape of design; inner edge will not lay flat. End of the tape should be covered by another layer; place end on top. (Right side of lace faces down.)

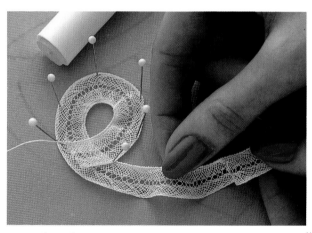

4) Push gathers up toward pinned area, easing and shaping inner curve so it lays flat. When tape is shaped, remove pins and apply glue stick to right side; repin, as necessary.

5) Repeat steps 3 and 4 for each loop or section. It may be helpful to remove pins from previous loops after glue has set.

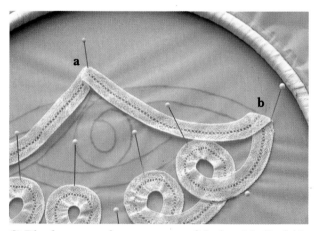

6) Pinch tape to shape corners of design **(a).** Or fold tape back on itself at corners **(b).**

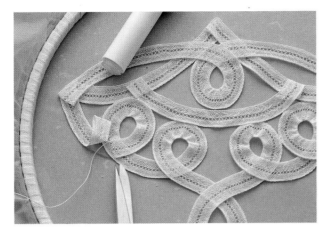

7) Trim excess tape, leaving ½" (1.3 cm) tail. Use additional pieces of tape, if necessary, to complete design. Fold under all ends of tape to secure and hide raw edges. Trim excess gimp. Remove pins.

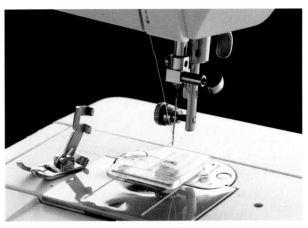

8) Thread the machine with embroidery thread; use same thread for needle and bobbin. Adjust machine for balanced tension (page 18). Cover the feed dogs with cover plate or lower them. Remove presser foot; lower presser foot lifter.

9) Stitch around outer edge of tape, using straight stitch; stitch through all layers where tape overlaps. (Contrasting thread was used to show detail.)

10) Secure edges of tape, where they abut, with three or four stitches, using straight-stitch zigzag. Do this by moving hoop slightly from side to side so needle catches first one side, then the other.

11) Continue stitching until all outer edges of tape are secure. Repeat for inner edges.

12) Sew desired fill-in stitches (pages 118 to 123) in open areas, using free-motion techniques; use machine embroidery thread in needle and bobbin.

Battenberg Fill-in Stitches

There are several kinds of fill-in stitches. Some of the traditional stitch patterns are (clockwise, starting at top) richelieu bars, point duchesse or Y-stitch, bundled bars, grid work, and spider web or windmill. The stitches may be combined in a Battenberg lace design (center).

There are two methods for making Battenberg stitches. One method uses the straight stitch and a technique referred to as *straight-stitch zigzag* to wrap the filler cords. For this method, the water-soluble stabilizer is removed from the centers of the loops before stitching; the stitching is then done without fabric under the needle of the machine.

The alternate method uses the zigzag stitch to wrap the filler cords; the water-soluble stabilizer is not removed until after the filler cords are wrapped. This method is used if the sewing machine skips stitches or jams when there is no fabric under the needle.

How to Sew Richelieu Bars

1) Remove stabilizer from center of loop. Mark dots on opposite sides of loop for each richelieu bar.

2) Draw up bobbin thread at dot for first richelieu bar; stitch in place a few times to secure stitches. Stitch to opposite dot and back about three times for filler cords, with each row of stitching beside previous row.

3) Stitch back over filler cords, using straight-stitch zigzag; do this by moving the hoop from side to side so stitches are taken on alternate sides of cords.

4) Stitch on tape to dot for next richelieu bar; repeat fill-in stitches for each bar. Secure the stitches after completing last bar.

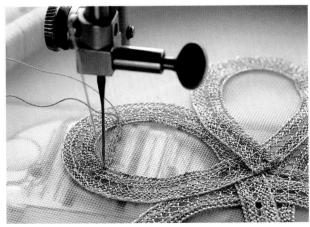

Alternate method. 1) Mark dots as in step 1, above, using water-soluble marking pen; do not remove stabilizer. Secure stitches; stitch filler cords for first bar, as in step 2, above.

2) Set machine for narrow zigzag. Stitch over filler cords; move hoop slowly and stitch at moderately fast speed for satin stitches. Straight-stitch on tape to dot for next richelieu bar; repeat fill-in stitches for each bar. Secure stitches after completing last bar.

How to Sew Point Duchesse Stitches or Y-stitches

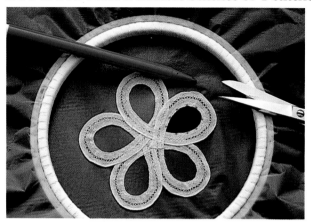

1) Remove the stabilizer from center of loop. Mark staggered dots on opposite sides of loop; dots should be no more than ¼" (6 mm) apart.

2) Draw up the bobbin thread at dot for first row; stitch in place a few times to secure stitches. Stitch to first dot on opposite side to make filler cord. Secure the stitches.

3) Stitch back over the filler cord for three or four stitches, using straight-stitch zigzag; do this by moving hoop from side to side so stitches are taken on alternate sides of cord.

4) Stitch to next dot on opposite side, stitching back over end of filler cord, as in step 3. Continue stitching in this manner to last dot. Secure stitches.

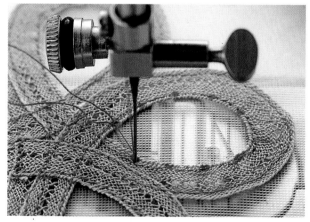

Alternate method. 1) Mark loop as in step 1, above; do not remove stabilizer. Draw up bobbin thread at dot for first row; secure stitches. Raise presser foot lifter and move hoop so threads pull across to first dot on opposite side to make filler cord; secure stitches.

2) Set machine for narrow zigzag; stitch back over thread for three or four stitches. Set machine for straight stitch; raise presser foot lifter and pull threads across to next dot on opposite side. Continue stitching in this manner to last dot; secure stitches.

How to Sew Bundled Bars

1) Remove stabilizer from center of loop. Mark top and bottom of loop; mark each side of loop into quarters. Make additional marks ⅛" (3 mm) on each side of quarter-marks.

2) Draw up bobbin thread at dot for first bar; stitch in place a few times to secure stitches. Stitch to opposite dot to make filler cord. Stitch back over filler cord, as in step 3, opposite.

3) Stitch on tape to dot for next bar; repeat fill-in stitches for each bar. Stitch on tape to dot at top of loop. Turn hoop one-quarter turn so bars are horizontal.

4) Stitch to first bar for center filler cord. Take one stitch over first three bars to pull them together.

5) Take one stitch back over bars to one side of center cord **(a).** Take one stitch over center cord to other side **(b).** Take one stitch back over all three bars **(c).**

6) Stitch to next group of bars and bundle them; repeat for last group of bars. Stitch to bottom of loop; secure stitches. Stitch over center filler cord, using straight-stitch zigzag. Secure stitches.

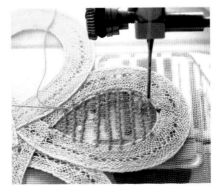

Alternate method. 1) Mark loop as in step 1, above; do not remove stabilizer. Draw up bobbin thread at dot for first bar; secure stitches. Straight-stitch to opposite dot to make filler cord. Stitch back over cord, using narrow zigzag. Stitch remaining bars. Secure stitches.

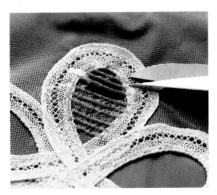

2) Remove hoop; trim stabilizer from loop, trimming close to bars and tape. Place a new layer of stabilizer under lace. Reposition in hoop.

3) Draw up bobbin thread at dot on top of loop; secure stitches. Straight-stitch to first bar for center filler cord. Push first and third bars toward center bar, using seam ripper; stitch over bars as in steps 4, 5, and 6. Stitch over center filler cord, using narrow zigzag. Secure stitches.

How to Sew Grid Work

1) Remove stabilizer from center of loop. Draw up bobbin thread; stitch in place a few times to secure stitches. Stitch across center of loop, using straight stitch; secure stitches. Stitch back over filler cord, using straight-stitch zigzag, as in step 3, page 119.

2) Stitch on tape for ¼" (6 mm). Stitch additional rows as in step 1, parallel to first row, keeping rows ¼" (6 mm) apart.

3) Stitch parallel rows, in the opposite direction, ¼" (6 mm) apart, as in step 1.

Alternate method. Stitch rows in both directions, as above, stitching across rows, using straight stitch, and back over rows, using narrow zigzag. Do not remove stabilizer before stitching.

How to Sew Spider Webs or Windmills

1) Remove stabilizer from center of loop. Mark top and bottom of loop; mark each side of loop into quarters. Draw up bobbin thread at dot at one end of loop; stitch in place a few times to secure stitches.

2) Stitch to opposite dot to make filler cord. Stitch back over filler cord, using straight-stitch zigzag, as in step 3, page 119. Stitch on tape to dot for next row.

3) Repeat fill-in stitches for two more rows, trying not to catch center of rows with needle. For last row, stitch to opposite dot to make filler cord and stitch back over filler cord, stopping at center.

4) Stitch around center intersection, inserting needle in each space between wrapped bars; stitch about four rows around center to build up web. Continue stitching over filler cord for last row; secure stitches.

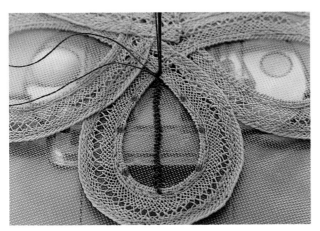

Alternate method. 1) Mark loop as in step 1, above; do not remove stabilizer. Secure stitches at dot at one end of loop. Stitch to opposite dot, using straight stitch. Set machine for narrow zigzag; stitch back over filler cords for first row.

2) Stitch on tape to dot for next row. Follow steps 3 and 4, above, for remaining rows, using narrow zigzag to stitch back over filler cords.

Applying Battenberg Lace to a Garment

Remove Battenberg lace from the embroidery hoop immediately after you have finished making it, to prevent any permanent distortion or creasing. To preshrink the lace before it is inserted in the garment, press it with a steam iron on a cotton setting.

For a neat edge finish on a lace insert, attach the outer edge to the garment, using a narrow zigzag stitch, and trim the garment fabric close to the stitching. Edges of necklines, collars, and cuffs may be trimmed with Battenberg tape. The tape is shaped around the garment edge and attached with zigzag stitching.

How to Finish Battenberg Lace

1) Remove lace from hoop as soon as design is completed. Carefully tear away as much of the water-soluble stabilizer as possible.

2) Soak lace in cool, soapy water for about five minutes to remove excess stabilizer, water-soluble pen marks, and glue. Pat the lace dry between layers of bath towel.

3) Place lace face down on padded surface; press with iron on cotton setting to shrink tape and threads.

How to Apply Battenberg Lace to a Garment

How to Finish Garment Edges

1) Pin finished lace to fabric in desired position. Uncover feed dogs or raise them. Attach presser foot. Stitch lace to garment on outer edge of tape, using narrow zigzag stitch.

2) Cut away fabric under the lace carefully, using embroidery scissors.

Place outer edge of tape along hemline or seamline; pin. Apply liquid fray preventer to ends of tape; turn under. Zigzag on inner edge; trim fabric close to stitches. Tack ends of tape by hand.

Index

Cy DeCosse Incorporated offers
sewing accessories to subscribers.
For information write:
  Sewing Accessories
  5900 Green Oak Drive
  Minnetonka, MN 55343